VOICES
FROM AMERICAN HISTORY

Program Consultants

Joseph D. Baca
Education Consultant
State Department of Education
Santa Fe, New Mexico

Catharine D. Bell
University of Chicago
Laboratory Schools
Chicago, Illinois

David L. Depew
Social Studies Consultant
Ector County Independent School District
Odessa, Texas

Miriam M. Glessner
Former Social Studies Supervisor
Columbus Public Schools
Columbus, Ohio

Gloria P. Hagans, Ed.D.
Social Studies Coordinator
Norfolk Public Schools
Norfolk, Virginia

Anthony La Rocca, M.S.
Social Studies Teacher
Bellmore, New York

Norman McRae, Ph.D.
Director, Fine Arts & Social Studies
Detroit Public Schools
Detroit, Michigan

Audrey Tieger, Ed.D.
President, California Council for the Social Studies
Los Angeles, California

Theron Trimble, Ed.D.
Social Studies Coordinator
Collier County Public Schools
Naples, Florida

STECK-VAUGHN COMPANY
A Subsidiary of National Education Corporation

Acknowledgments

Executive Editor: Elizabeth Strauss

Project Editor: Anne Souby

Product Development: Learning Design Associates, Inc.

Cover Design: Joyce Spicer

Cover Artist: Susan Melrath

VOICES Series

Level E/Voices From Our Country
Level F/Voices From World History
Level G/Voices From World Geography
Level H/Voices From American History

The credits and acknowledgments that appear following each reading and on page 124 of this book are hereby made a part of this copyright page.

ISBN 0-8114-4456-2

Copyright © 1991 Steck-Vaughn Company.
All rights reserved. No part of the material protected by this copyright may be reproduced or utilized in any form or by any means, electronic or mechanical, including photocopying, recording, or by any information storage and retrieval system, without permission in writing from the copyright owner. Requests for permission to make copies of any part of the work should be mailed to:
Copyright Permissions, Steck-Vaughn Company,
P.O. Box 26015, Austin, TX 78755.

Printed in the United States of America.

1 2 3 4 5 6 7 8 9 0 DP 95 94 93 92 91 90

CONTENTS

Unit 1 — Routes to a New World

The Admiral's Letter
  Christopher Columbus writes about his trip to the Indies 4
Vespucci's New World   *Amerigo Vespucci reports on the new continent* 8
Riding With Coronado
  A Spanish soldier describes the American Southwest 12

Unit 2 — Settlers of the Northern Colonies

News From New England
  A Pilgrim describes life in Plymouth Colony 16
The Puritan Way   *Two colonists reveal Puritan lifestyles* 18
A Land of Opportunity?
  A German visitor writes of the lives of indentured servants 22

Unit 3 — Birth of a Nation

A Taxing Problem
  Benjamin Franklin testifies before England's Parliament 28
Wounded in Action
  A woman disguised as a man fights in the Revolutionary War 32
Colonial Soldier   *A black Revolutionary War veteran requests a pension* 34

Unit 4 — On the Move

Gold Rush Diary   *A '49er mines for gold in California* 38
Diary of an Oregon Pioneer
  A young woman describes life on the Oregon Trail 42
Wrapped in Straw and Boxed Up
  How one slave ships himself north to freedom 46

Unit 5 — The Civil War

Gettysburg Diary
  A Union soldier writes about the bloody Battle of Gettysburg 52
When Sherman Marched
  A Southern woman comes face-to-face with Sherman's army 54
Surrender at Appomattox   *Ulysses S. Grant meets Robert E. Lee* 58

Unit 6   The Changing Frontier

Driving the Golden Spike
A journalist reports on the first transcontinental railroad 64

Justice for All
Chief Red Cloud addresses a New York City audience 66

Cowboy Style   *A former cowboy remembers life in the American West* 68

Unit 7   Reforms in a New Century

Guilty of Voting
Susan B. Anthony testifies before a court of law 72

A Brief Sketch of My Life
George Washington Carver relates his rise from slavery 76

The Jungle   *Upton Sinclair describes conditions in the meat-packing industry* 80

Unit 8   World in Crisis

The Push Forward   *A soldier writes a letter home from the trenches of France* 86

This I Remember
Eleanor Roosevelt visits a West Virginia mining town 88

Hard Times
A migrant worker remembers the Great Depression 90

Unit 9   Allies in Arms

Women in the War Effort
One "Rosie the Riveter" tells how she did her part for the war effort 96

Normandy Invasion   *Journalist Ernie Pyle reports from the front lines* 100

Impressions of Dachau
An American officer helps liberate a Nazi concentration camp 106

Unit 10   Call for Equality

The Black Eagle Is Born
Cesar Chavez remembers organizing America's farm workers 110

I Have a Dream   *Dr. Martin Luther King, Jr., delivers his inspirational speech* 112

Women in Leadership
Congresswoman Geraldine Ferraro addresses women's issues 118

INTRODUCTION

America's history is the story of many men and women. Some are great historical figures who have shaped the course of America's development. Others are everyday people caught up in momentous events. Their struggles and successes are the very essence of America.

The best way to learn about history is to listen to the people who lived it. In *Voices* people from the past speak in their own words—about their lives and the time they lived in. Through their letters, diaries, speeches, and memoirs, you'll hear their voices. You'll learn about their thoughts, lives, feelings, and dreams. *Voices* is a tapestry of living history.

In these pages you can read Christopher Columbus's letter to the Spanish court describing the Indies. Witness Benjamin Franklin's formal plea to the British Parliament to repeal the Stamp Act. Share a slave's perilous escape to freedom via the Underground Railroad. Observe General Lee's surrender at Appomattox. Witness the final spike being driven into the transcontinental railroad. Feel the emotion of Susan B. Anthony's defense of her (then illegal) attempt to vote. Experience the stirring "I Have a Dream" speech of Dr. Martin Luther King, Jr. Collectively these firsthand accounts illuminate the entire spectrum of American history.

Each reading starts with a short introduction. This paragraph helps to set the scene. The paragraph at the end of each reading reveals what happened next. Timelines and maps pinpoint the sequence and location of events. Margin notes define unfamiliar words.

These first-person narratives provide a moving eyewitness account of American history. They are eloquent voices from our past that still speak to us today.

UNIT 1

ROUTES TO A NEW WORLD

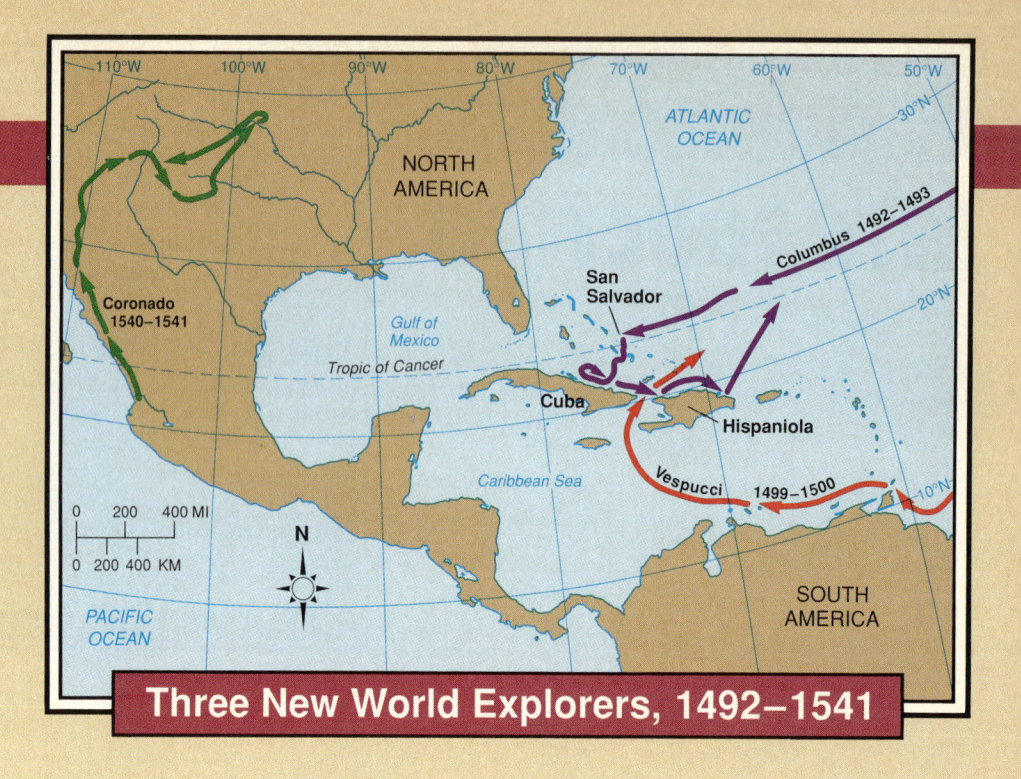

Three New World Explorers, 1492–1541

Europeans enjoyed the wonderful silks, spices, and precious metals that came overland from India, China, and Southeast Asia. But these luxuries were expensive, and a water route to Asia was needed to make them less costly. Christopher Columbus was certain that a water route to Asia lay to the west, across the Atlantic Ocean. In 1492, with three vessels and 90 sailors, Columbus embarked on a trip that he believed would last three weeks. He did not know he had just begun a perilous journey that would take him across thousands of miles of uncharted Atlantic waters.

The three-week trip Columbus had promised dragged into four weeks, five weeks, six weeks. Still no land was in sight. Every day the sailors saw nothing but green ocean and blue sky. Supplies ran low; the crew became mutinous. Then one night—the evening of October 12, 1492—the ship's lookout spotted moonlight reflecting off a sandy shore. Land! After two months at sea Columbus had discovered what he thought was the Indies. He returned to Spain believing—and claiming —that he had discovered a route to the Far East.

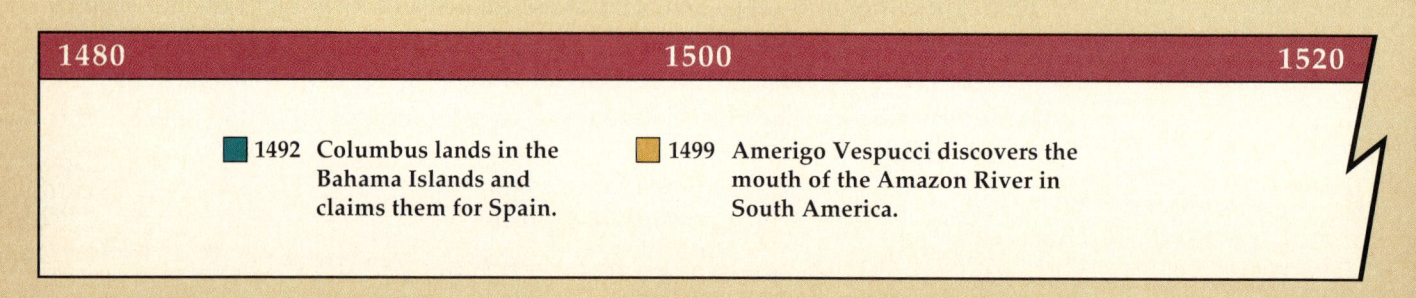

1480	1500	1520

- **1492** Columbus lands in the Bahama Islands and claims them for Spain.
- **1499** Amerigo Vespucci discovers the mouth of the Amazon River in South America.

Other explorers from many different countries followed in Columbus's wake. One of these was the Italian-born Amerigo Vespucci, who was commissioned by Spain and Portugal. Vespucci was the first explorer to determine that these new lands were not a part of Asia at all but were part of a previously undiscovered landmass. The new continents, the Americas, were named in his honor.

In the years that followed, explorers extended their search inland for riches and adventure. Francisco de Coronado traveled through what is now the southwestern United States in search of the mythical seven golden cities of Cíbola. He found no gold, but, like other explorers of his age, he added much to Europeans' knowledge of the New World.

On his first voyage Columbus gathered plants and artifacts to bring back to the queen and king of Spain. He even persuaded a few Native Americans to make the return trip.

In this unit three European explorers describe the New World as they first saw it.

- **Christopher Columbus** writes about his trip to the Indies in a letter to a Spanish official.
- In a letter **Amerigo Vespucci** describes his first voyage and his sighting of a new continent.
- Pedro de Castañeda, one of **Francisco de Coronado's** soldiers, writes in his journal of a visit to a Native American settlement in the American Southwest.

| 1540 | 1560 |

1541 Francisco de Coronado explores what is now the southwestern United States.

3

The Admiral's Letter

" There are spices and great mines of gold and other metals."
Christopher Columbus

Explorer Christopher Columbus points out his discoveries in the New World to Queen Isabella and King Ferdinand of Spain.

Christopher Columbus was attracted to the riches of the Far East. Like others of the time he believed the world was round. The riches of China, he thought, could be reached by sailing westward from Europe. Columbus persuaded the king and queen of Spain to finance a westward voyage and to give him a share of profits from trade. In this letter written in 1493 to an official of the Spanish royal court, Columbus reports his discovery of "the **Indies**."

Indies: West Indies. Columbus, however, believed he had reached the East Indies, in Asia.

Canary Islands: islands in the Atlantic Ocean, near the northwest coast of Africa

illustrious: very famous, outstanding

proclamation: official announcement

gainsay: go against or deny

Juana: now Cuba

SIR:

As I know you will take pleasure in the great victory Our Lord has given me in my voyage, I write this so you will learn how I went over from the **Canary Islands** to the Indies in thirty-three days with the fleet that the most **illustrious** King and Queen, our lords, gave me, where I found very many islands inhabited by people without number. I have taken possession of them all for Their Highnesses by **proclamation**, with royal banner unfurled and no one to **gainsay** me. To the first island that I found, I gave the name San Salvador, in remembrance of the Divine Majesty who marvelously has given all this. The Indians call it Guanahaní. To the second, I gave the name Santa María de la Concepción, to the third, Fernandina, to the fourth, Isabella, the fifth, **Juana**, and so to each one I gave a new name.

1492	
1492 On his first voyage to the New World, Columbus reaches San Salvador while in search of a short route to the Indies.	1493 Columbus explores Cuba, Hispaniola, Jamaica, and Puerto Rico on his second voyage.

When I reached Juana, I followed the coast to the westward, and found it so large that I thought it must be the mainland, the province of **Cathay**. And since I found neither towns or villages on the seashore, only small **hamlets**, with whose people I could not speak, as they all fled, I went forward on the same course, thinking I should not fail to find great cities and towns. At the end of many **leagues,** seeing there was no change and the coast carried me northward, where I did not want to go, as winter was beginning and I proposed to escape it by going south, I retraced my course to a harbor I had noticed on the way. . . .

I understood well enough from other Indians I had already taken that this was an island. Therefore, I followed the coast eastward for 107 leagues to the point where it ended. And from there I saw another island to the east at a distance of eighteen leagues, to which I at once gave the name Hispaniola. I went there and followed the northern coast as I had done on Juana. This island and the others are unbelievably fertile, Hispaniola especially. There are many harbors on the coast, better than any I know in **Christendom**, and many rivers, good and large. Its land rises from the sea and there are very many **sierras** and lofty mountains. All are beautiful, of a thousand shapes, and all **accessible.** They are filled with trees of a thousand kinds, so tall they seem to touch the sky. I am

Cathay: China

hamlets: small villages

leagues: measurement of distance equaling about three miles

Christendom: Christian part of the world; Europe

sierras: chains of hills or mountains with jagged peaks

accessible: easy to reach

Ferdinand and Isabella gave Columbus this "Book of Privileges" as part of his agreement to explore for Spain. His privileges included a share in trade and the title of admiral.

| 1498 | On his third voyage Columbus reaches the northern coast of South America. | 1502 | Columbus explores the coast of Central America on his fourth and final voyage to the New World. |

Many of the inhabitants of the West Indies welcomed Columbus on his first journey. Not all remained friendly when they realized that Spain was interested in their gold and land.

told they never lose their leaves, which I can understand, as I saw them as green and beautiful as they are in Spain in May.... There are marvelous pine groves, large open fields, honey, birds of many kinds and a great variety of fruits. Inland there are many mines and people without number. Hispaniola is a marvel.

The sierras and mountains, the plains, fields, and pastures are lovely and rich for planting and sowing, for breeding livestock of all kinds, for building towns and villages. The harbors cannot be believed without seeing them, and so with the rivers, many and great, and good streams, the majority of them bearing gold. There are spices and great mines of gold and other metals.

The people of this island and the others that I have found, both men and women, go naked as their mothers bore them.... They have no other **arms** than those made from canes cut at seed time, on the end of which they fix a small sharpened stick—and they do not dare to use these. Many times I have sent two or three men ashore to talk to them, and great numbers of people have come out. As soon as they have seen my men nearing, they have fled, even a father not waiting for his son. And this not because harm has been done to anyone. On the contrary, at every point where I have been and been able to talk to them, I have given them all that I had, such as cloth and other things, without getting anything in return. But they are like that, hopelessly timid. It is true that after they have been reassured and have lost their fear, they are so **artless** and so generous with all they have, that no one would believe it who has not seen it. They never say no when asked for anything they own. On the contrary, they invite everybody to share it.... I forbade that they should be given things so worthless as pieces of broken **crockery** and scraps of glass, and ends of straps, although when they got them they thought they had the best jewel in the world. So it was found that a sailor got two and one-half *castellanos* weight of gold for a strap and others much

arms: weapons

artless: natural, without tricks or lies

crockery: pots, jars, or dishes made of baked clay

castellanos: Spanish coins

more for other things worth much less. They even took pieces of hoops of wine barrels, and like animals, gave what they had, so that it seemed wrong to me, and I stopped it.

And I gave a thousand good, pleasing things I had brought so they might like us, and more than that, might become Christians and be inclined to the love and service of Their Highnesses and the whole **Castilian** nation, and strive to help us and give us some of the things they have in abundance and which we need. They do not know any **creed** nor are they **idolaters**, only they all believe that power and good are in the sky, and they firmly believe that I, these ships and men, came from the sky. And this does not come from their being ignorant. On the contrary, they have a very keen intelligence. They can navigate all those seas and it is amazing how good an account they give of everything. It is because they have never seen people wearing clothes, or ships like ours.

As soon as I arrived in the Indies, on the first island, I took some of them by force, so that they might learn and give me information about these parts. They soon understood us and we them, either by speech or signs, and they have been very **serviceable**. I still have them with me and they still think I come from the sky. They were the first to announce this wherever I went, and the others went running from house to house and to the neighboring towns with the loud cries of "Come! Come! See the people from the sky!"

In conclusion, to speak only of that which has been accomplished on this voyage, which was so hasty, Their Highnesses can see that I will give them all the gold they want if Their Highnesses will give me a little help, and I will give them spice and cotton too, as much as Their Highnesses shall command. And I shall find a thousand other things of value, which the men I left behind have found by now.

This is enough. And the eternal God, Our Lord, gives to all those who walk in His way triumph over things which appear impossible, and this was **notably** one. . . .

Done in the **caravel**, off the **Azores**, on the fifteenth of February, 1493.

At your service,
The Admiral

Castilian: Spanish. Castile was another name for Spain.

creed: religious belief

idolaters: people who worship idols

serviceable: useful

notably: especially

caravel: small, fast sailing ship

Azores: group of islands in the Atlantic Ocean, west of Portugal

---

Queen Isabella and her husband Ferdinand financed three more voyages, but Columbus never found the riches that he had expected. In fact, he returned in chains from his third voyage because he refused to obey orders sent by the king and queen. Columbus later made one more voyage, landing in **Honduras**. He died in Spain at age 55, still believing that he had found the westward route to Asia.

Honduras: country in Central America

From *The Quest of Columbus*, pp. 103–7, edited and adapted by Robert Meredith and E. Brooks Smith. Copyright © 1966 by Robert K. Meredith and Edric B. Smith, Jr. By permission of Little, Brown and Company.

Vespucci's New World

" . . . we sailed on till at the end of 37 days we reached a land which we deemed to be a continent. . . ."

Amerigo Vespucci

Amerigo Vespucci may have been the first European explorer to realize that he had found a new continent.

Amerigo Vespucci was a merchant who worked for the company that supplied Columbus's second and third expeditions to the New World. Perhaps inspired by Columbus's voyages, Vespucci took part in other expeditions across the ocean. In a letter to an Italian noble, Vespucci describes a trip he claims to have made in 1497. He writes that he discovered the mainland of a new continent that was full of people and wild animals.

> Magnificent Lord. . . . The chief cause which moved (*me*) to write to you, was at the request of the present bearer, who is named Benvenuto Benvenuti our Florentine (*fellow-citizen*), very much, as it is proven, your Magnificence's servant, and my very good friend: who happening to be here in this city of Lisbon, begged that I should make communication to your Magnificence of the things seen by me in divers regions of the world, by virtue of four voyages which I have made in discovery of new lands. . . . So may you, for a relief from your so heavy occupations, order this letter of mine to be read: so that they may withdraw you somewhat from the **continual anxiety** and **assiduous reflection** upon public affairs. . . . Your Magnificence shall know that the motive of my coming into this realm of Spain was to **traffic** in merchandise: and that I pursued this intent about four years. . . . I **resolved** to abandon trade, and to fix my

continual anxiety: unending worry

assiduous reflection: careful thinking

traffic: do business

resolved: was determined

1499

1499 Vespucci sails from Spain to the coast of South America, where he discovers the mouth of the Amazon River.

1501 Vespucci sails from Portugal to the coast of Brazil. He travels along its eastern coast as far south as Patagonia.

aim upon something more praiseworthy and stable. . . . The King Don Ferrando of Castile being about to **despatch** four ships to discover new lands towards the west, I was chosen by his Highness to go in that fleet to aid in making discovery: and we set out from the port of **Cadiz** on the 10th day of May 1497, and took our route through the great **gulph** of the Ocean-sea; in which voyage we were eighteen months (*engaged*): and discovered much continental land and innumerable islands, and great part of them inhabited. . . . We left the port of Cadiz four **consort** ships: and began our voyage in direct course to the **Fortunate Isles** which are called to-day *la gran Canaria*. . . . We remained eight days, taking in provision of water, and wood and other necessary things: and from here, having said our prayers, we **weighed anchor**, and gave the sails to the wind, beginning our course to westward . . . we sailed on till at the end of 37 days we reached a land which we **deemed** to be a continent. . . . This land is very populous, and full of inhabitants, and of numberless rivers, (*and*) animals: few (*of which*) resemble ours, excepting lions, panthers, stags, pigs, goats, and deer: and even these have some dissimilarities of form: they have no horses nor mules, nor, **saving your reverence**, asses nor dogs, nor any kind of sheep or oxen: but so numerous are the other animals which they have, and all are savage, and of

despatch: (dispatch) send

Cadiz: seaport in southwestern Spain

gulph: (gulf)

consort: accompanying

Fortunate Isles: Canary Islands in the Atlantic Ocean off the northwest coast of Africa

weighed anchor: raised the anchor

deemed: thought

saving your reverence: with all due respect

Vespucci was a skilled navigator. In this engraving he is studying the four stars of the Southern Cross, a constellation in the sky of the Southern Hemisphere.

1507 A German mapmaker suggests the New World be named "America" in honor of Vespucci.

1508 Vespucci is made chief navigator of Spain. His duties include preparing maps of newly discovered land and interpreting information provided by ships' captains.

9

Vespucci was not always welcomed by the people who inhabited the continent of South America.

plumages: feathers

foliage: leaves

torrid zone: very warm region between the Tropic of Cancer and the Tropic of Capricorn; also known as the tropics

pole of the horizon, extremity of the second climate: 23°N latitude

whence: from where

tackling: ropes that raise the sails

stanching: (staunching) stopping

caulking: filling up cracks to make them watertight

victuals: food

none do they make use for their service, that they could not be counted. What shall we say of others (*such as*) birds? which are so numerous, and of so many kinds, and of such various-coloured **plumages,** that it is a marvel to behold them. The soil is very pleasant and fruitful, full of immense woods and forests: and it is always green, for the **foliage** never drops off. The fruits are so many that they are numberless and entirely different from ours. This land is within the **torrid zone**, close to or just under the parallel described by the Tropic of Cancer: where the **pole of the horizon** has an elevation of 23 degrees, at the **extremity of the second climate**. Many tribes came to see us, and wondered at our faces and our whiteness: and they asked us **whence** we came: and we gave them to understand that we had come from heaven, and that we were going to see the world, and they believed it.... We had now been thirteen months on the voyage: and the vessels and the **tackling** were already much damaged, and the men worn out by fatigue: we decided by general council to haul our ships on land and examine them for the purpose of **stanching** leaks, as they made much water, and of **caulking** and tarring them afresh, and (*then*) returning towards Spain: and when we came to this determination, we were close to a harbour the best in the world: into which we entered with our vessels: where we found an immense number of people: who received us with much friendliness.... Our ships having been unloaded and lightened, we drew them upon land, and repaired them in everything that was needful: and the land's people gave us very great assistance: and continually furnished us with their **victuals**: so that in this port we tasted little of our own, which suited our game well: for the stock of provisions which we had for our return-passage was little and of sorry kind: where (*i.e., there*) we remained 37 days: and went many times to their villages: where they paid us the greatest honour.... Many of them offered to come along with us, but we did not wish to take them for many reasons, **save** that we took seven of them.... And so we departed from those people, leaving them very friendly towards us: and having repaired our ships, and sailing for seven days out to sea between northeast and east: and at the end of the seven days we came upon the islands, which were many, some (*of them*) inhabited, and others deserted: and we anchored at one of them: where we saw a numerous people who called it Iti: and having manned our boats with strong crews, and (*taken ammunition for*) three cannon-shots in each, we made for land: where we found (*assembled*) about 400 men, and many women, and all naked like the former (*peoples*). They were of good bodily presence, and seemed right warlike men: for they were armed with their weapons, which are bows, arrows, and lances: and most of them had square wooden **targets**: and bore them in such **wise** that they did not **impede** the drawing of the bow: and when we had come with our boats to about a bowshot of the land, they all sprang into the water to shoot their arrows at us and to prevent us from leaping upon shore.... They advanced towards us, and we fought for about an hour, for we had but little advantage of them, except that our **arbalasters** and gunners killed some of them, and they wounded certain of our men.... At last that we came to sword-play, and when they **tasted our weapons**, they **betook** themselves to flight through the mountains and the forests, and left us conquerors of the field with many of them dead and a good number wounded.... Of ours there were no more than one killed, and 22 wounded, who all escaped (*i.e., recovered*), God be thanked. We arranged our departure, and seven men, of whom five were wounded, took an island-canoe, and with seven prisoners that we gave them, four women and three men, returned to their (*own*) country full of gladness, wondering at our strength: and we thereon made sail for Spain with 222 captive slaves: and reached the port of Calis (*Cadiz*) on the 15th day of October, 1498, where we were well received and sold our slaves. Such is what **befell** me, most noteworthy, in this my first voyage.

save: except

targets: shields

wise: way or manner

impede: get in the way of, obstruct

arbalasters: men who shot crossbows

tasted our weapons: saw the effect of our weapons

betook: went

befell: happened to

The number and dates of Vespucci's voyages to the New World are disputed today. Some historians believe that Vespucci never made a voyage in 1497. Most agree, however, that he was present on at least two expeditions, one in 1499 and another in 1501. He explored the eastern coast of South America, a land he believed made up a new continent or "new world." It was Amerigo Vespucci's description of the newly discovered land that caused a mapmaker to call the continent "America."

From *American Historical Documents* (Vol.43), ed. Charles W. Eliot (New York: P. F. Collier & Son, 1910), pp. 29–32, 42–46. Reprinted with permission of *The Harvard Classics*. Copyright © Grolier Inc.

Riding With Coronado

" The people of this village boast that no one has been able to conquer them. . . ."
Pedro de Castañeda

Francisco de Coronado marched through the Southwest with 500 Spanish soldiers and hundreds of Native Americans.

The Native Americans in Central America told fantastic tales of seven cities of gold. If a Spanish explorer found such riches, he would bring fame and fortune to himself and glory to Spain. Francisco de Coronado marched north from Mexico in 1540 in search of the riches. One of Coronado's soldiers, Pedro de Castañeda, wrote in his journal about the kind of riches they found and the people they met.

Cicuye: present-day Pecos, New Mexico

pueblo: Native American village with houses built of adobe and stone, usually built one above the other

council chambers: place where the tribal rulers meet

Cicuye is a village of nearly five hundred warriors, who are feared throughout that country. The **pueblo** is square, situated on a rock, with a large courtyard in the middle containing underground **council chambers.** The houses are all alike, four stories high. One can go over the top of the whole village without a street to stop him. There are corridors going all around it at the first two stories. These are like outside balconies, and they are able to protect themselves under them. The houses do not have doors below. They use ladders, which can be lifted up like a drawbridge to the corridors inside the village. As the doors of the houses open on the corridor. . . the corridor serves as a street. . . . In time of war the people in the outside houses go through those on the court. The village is enclosed by a low wall of stone. There is a spring of water inside.

The people of this village boast that no one has been able to conquer them and they conquer whatever villages they wish. . . . Cicuye is in a little valley between mountain chains and mountains covered with pine forests. There is a little stream which contains very good trout and otters,

1535

1535 Coronado sails to Mexico from Spain. He becomes governor of a Mexican province.

and there are very large bears and good falcons hereabouts.

Near Cicuye is **another village** almost deserted. This was a large village and seemed to have been almost destroyed by attackers.... Another large village farther on had been entirely destroyed and pulled down. All that I was able to find out about them was that sixteen years before some people called **Teyas** had come to this country in great numbers and had destroyed the villages. They had **besieged** Cicuye but had not been able to capture it because it was strong. When they left, they had made peace with the whole country.

They must have been a powerful people. The only thing the people of Cicuye could tell about where they came from was by pointing toward the north.... The Teyas come from the plains to spend the winter under the wings of the villages. The inhabitants do not dare to let them come inside because they do not trust them. Although the Teyas are received as friends, and trade with them, they do not stay in the villages overnight, but outside under the wings. The villages are guarded by **sentinels** with trumpets who call to one another just as in the fortresses of Spain.

another village: called the village of the silos because of its large underground cellars filled with corn

Teyas: Texas tribe; called "brave men" by the people of Cicuye

besieged: surrounded in order to force a surrender

sentinels: people who keep watch to guard a group against surprise attacks

Zuñi women were skilled basket weavers and potters. Each Zuñi pueblo had its own unique pottery design.

In search of the cities whose streets were paved with gold, Coronado explored present-day New Mexico. Instead of cities of gold Coronado found **Zuñi** pueblos. Coronado and his men then crossed the Texas panhandle and Oklahoma, reaching eastern Kansas. When Coronado returned to Mexico in 1542, he thought that his journey had been a failure. He did not realize that he had opened the American Southwest to Spain.

Zuñi: Native Americans of the Pueblo group who live in western New Mexico

From *Riding With Coronado*, pp. 44–45, adapted and edited by Robert Meredith and Edric B. Smith, Jr. Copyright © 1964 by Edric B. Smith, Jr. and Robert K. Meredith. By permission of Little, Brown and Company.

1540	1541	1542
Coronado leads an expedition in search of the seven cities of gold to claim their wealth for Spain.	Coronado's expedition reaches Kansas, where they find a village, but no gold.	Coronado returns to Mexico without finding gold.

13

SETTLERS OF THE NORTHERN COLONIES

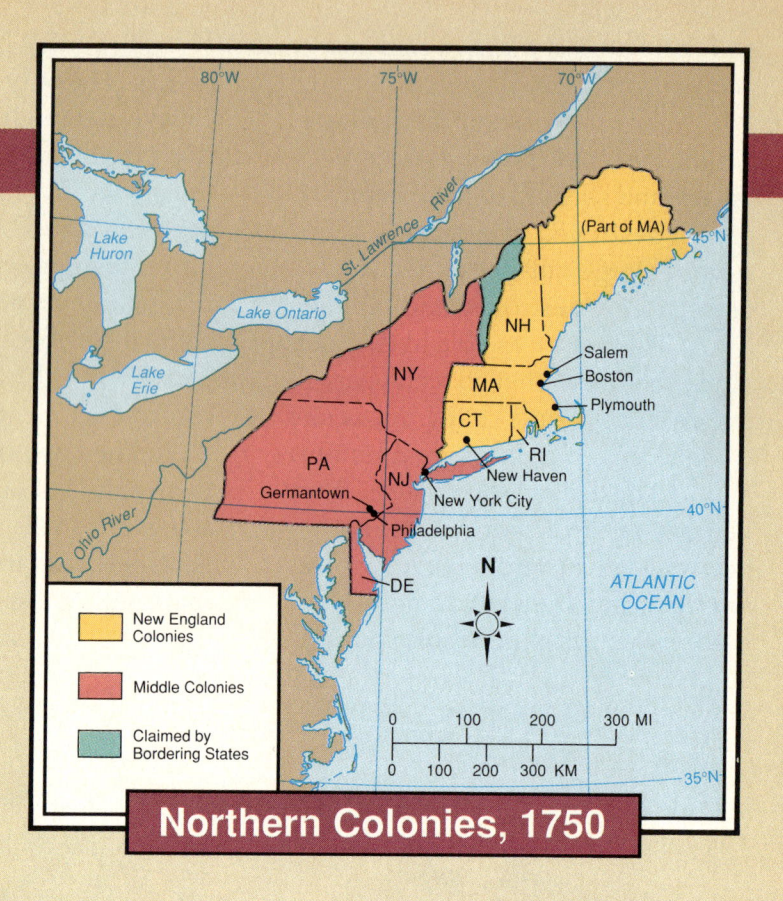

Northern Colonies, 1750

In 1620 two ships set sail on a voyage from England to the New World. Just out of port the *Speedwell* proved unseaworthy and many of its Pilgrim passengers crowded onto the decks of the companion ship, the *Mayflower*. So began a perilous two-month journey across the Atlantic Ocean—a journey that ended at Plymouth.

The delays at the onset cost the Pilgrims dearly by the voyage's end. As the *Mayflower* neared America's coast, the air turned crisp, and ocean spray froze on the crew's clothing. By the time the Pilgrims came ashore at Plymouth, winter already had a firm grip on the land and its new inhabitants.

Unloading the ship and building shelters proved to be difficult tasks in the frigid weather. In addition, food was scarce, for the Pilgrims had arrived ill-equipped for their new home. Their fishing hooks were too large for many of the area's fish, and the Pilgrims were not yet skilled in the use of their muskets. Life in the new land was so harsh that almost half of the settlers did not live to see springtime in Plymouth.

| 1620 | 1650 | 1680 |

■ 1621 Edward Winslow writes a letter describing the Pilgrim's first year in Plymouth Colony.

The Puritans, who accounted for about a third of the *Mayflower's* passengers, sought the religious freedom they had not found in their homeland. They believed in hard work, a simple life, and strict adherence to Puritan beliefs. One Sunday early that first winter, a storm blew the roof off the meetinghouse. Rather than repair the roof—and break their rule against working on the Sabbath—the Puritans continued their prayers as snow and sleet fell on their bowed heads.

The *Mayflower* also carried some of America's first indentured servants. These were poor people from Europe who could not afford to pay the passage to America. After their work contracts were completed, most received a suit of clothing, tools, and 50 acres of land. The thousands of indentured servants who came to the New World, with their hard work and sacrifice, helped build America.

The first European settlers in North America forged alliances with Native Americans to ensure peace and learn how to survive hardships in this new land.

In this unit four early settlers describe colonial American life.

- **Edward Winslow**, in a letter to a friend in England, describes his first year in Plymouth Colony.
- Both **Mary Osgood Sumner's** diary and **Joseph Bennett's** description of the Sabbath highlight the Puritan way of life.
- **Gottlieb Mittelberger's** article and the runaway notices provide insight into the lives of indentured servants.

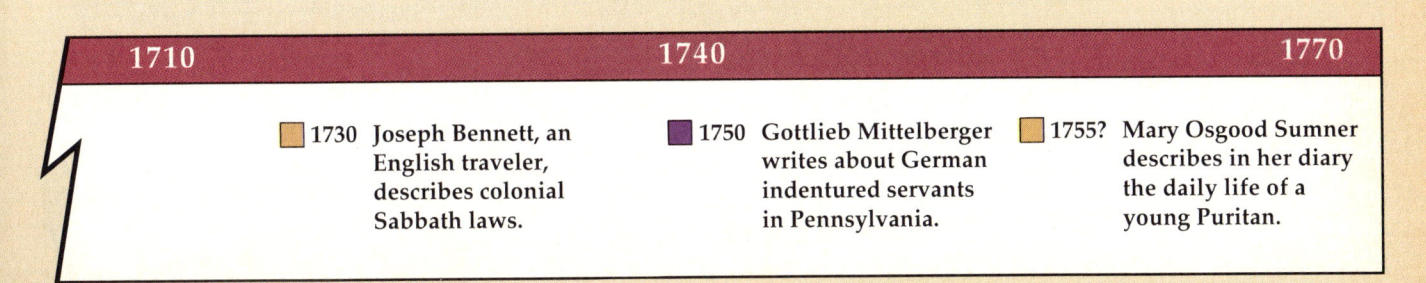

1710	1740	1770
1730 Joseph Bennett, an English traveler, describes colonial Sabbath laws.	1750 Gottlieb Mittelberger writes about German indentured servants in Pennsylvania.	1755? Mary Osgood Sumner describes in her diary the daily life of a young Puritan.

15

News From New England

> " I never in my life remember a more seasonable year than we have here enjoyed...."
>
> Edward Winslow

Chief Massasoit befriended the Pilgrims soon after they arrived at Plymouth. He made a peace agreement with Governor John Carver.

The Pilgrims came to America seeking religious freedom. They suffered many hardships in settling this unfamiliar land. The long voyage across the Atlantic Ocean had weakened them. Their first winter in America was very difficult, and by spring many had died from hunger and disease. Despite the hardships E.W., probably Edward Winslow, describes a land of beauty. The spellings and sentence structure in this letter reflect those of the time.

this ship: the *Fortune,* the first ship to follow the *Mayflower*

plantation: settlement

divers: (diverse) several

pease: (peas)

manured: fertilized

shads: a kind of fish

covenant: formal agreement; contract

Loving and Old Friend,

Although I received no letter from you by **this ship**, yet forasmuch as I know you expect the performance of my promise, which was, to write unto you truly and faithfully of all things, I have therefore at this time sent unto you accordingly....

You shall understand that in this little time that a few of us have been here, we have built seven dwelling-houses, and four for the use of the **plantation**, and have made preparation for **divers** others. We set the last spring some twenty acres of Indian corn, and sowed some six acres of barley and **pease**, and according to the manner of the Indians, we **manured** our ground with herrings, or rather **shads**, which we have in great abundance....

We have found the Indians very faithful in their **covenant** of peace with us.... Yea, it hath pleased God so to possess the Indians with a fear

1607

1607 England's first permanent colony is established in what is now Virginia.

of us, and love unto us, that not only the greatest king amongst them, called **Massasoit**, but also all the princes and peoples round about us, have either **made suit** unto us, or been glad of any occasion to make peace with us, so that seven of them at once have sent their messengers to us to that end. . . . We entertain them familiarly in our houses, and they as friendly **bestowing** their venison on us. . . .

For the temper of the air, here it agreeth well with that in England, and if there be any difference at all, this is somewhat hotter in summer. Some think it to be colder in winter, but I cannot out of experience so say; the air is very clear and not foggy, as hath been reported. I never in my life remember a more seasonable year than we have here enjoyed. . . . For fish and fowl, we have great abundance; fresh cod in the summer is but **coarse meat** with us; our bay is full of lobsters all the summer and **affordeth** variety of other fish; in September we can take a **hogshead** of eels in a night, with small labor, and can dig them out of their beds all the winter. . . . All the spring-time the earth sendeth forth naturally very good **sallet herbs**. Here are grapes, white and red, and very sweet and strong also. Strawberries, gooseberries, **raspas**, etc. Plums of three sorts, with black and red, being almost as good as a **damson**; abundance of roses, white, red, and **damask**; single, but very sweet indeed. . . .

I **forbear** further to write for the present, hoping to see you by the next return, so I take my leave, commending you to the Lord for a safe conduct unto us. Resting in him,

Your loving friend,
E. W.

Plymouth, in New England, this 11th of December, 1621.

Massasoit: Native American chief

made suit: made a request

bestowing: giving as a gift

coarse meat: food of poor quality; common food

affordeth: gives

hogshead: barrel; about 63 gallons

sallet herbs: salad greens

raspas: raspberries

damson: small purple plum

damask: deep pink or rose color

forbear: cease

Edward Winslow's *Good News From New England* was published in London in 1624. The book gave a personal account of the early years in the Plymouth Colony. The Pilgrims survived the first years with help from the Native Americans and through their own hard work. In 1629 other Puritans founded the Massachusetts Bay Colony, which grew quickly. Plymouth, however, remained small and in 1686 became part of Massachusetts Bay.

From *A Journal of the Pilgrims at Plymouth: Mourt's Relation*, pp. 81–84, 86–87, edited by Dwight B. Heath. Copyright © 1963 by Dwight B. Heath. Published by arrangement with Carol Publishing Group.

| 1620 Plymouth Colony is founded by Pilgrims. | 1621 Many Pilgrims die during the first winter. Native Americans help the survivors. |

The Puritan Way

"I went to meeting and paid good attention to the sermon...."
    Mary Osgood Sumner

With Bibles in hand Puritans walk through the snow on their way to Sunday church service at the village meetinghouse.

The Puritans who came to America wanted total obedience to their church. They were punished for doing chores or playing on the Sabbath. Strict rules guided every part of life. Puritans stressed education and hard work. In her diary Mary Osgood Sumner outlines her good and bad behaviors as a child attending Midway Church. Joseph Bennett tells about colonial Sabbath laws in a New England town in the 1730s.

Diary of Mary Osgood Sumner

Black Leaf: list of Sumner's wrongdoings

staise: (stays) bone strips used to give garments a stiff form

frock: dress

diligent: hard-working; careful

vexed: annoyed

Black Leaf
July 8. I left my **staise** on the bed.
"   9. Misplaced Sister's sash.
"   10. Spoke in haste to my little Sister, spilt the cream on the floor in the closet.
"   12. I left Sister Cynthia's **frock** on the bed.
"   16. I left the brush on the chair; was not **diligent** in learning at school.
"   17. I left my fan on the bed.
"   19. I got **vexed** because Sister was a-going to cut my frock.
"   22. Part of this day I did not improve my time well.
"   30. I was careless and lost my needle.
Aug. 5. I spilt some coffee on the table.

1630

1630 Puritans settle in the Massachusetts Bay Colony.

1636 Puritans start the first college in the colonies.

1642 A Puritan law is enacted that requires parents to teach their children how to read.

White Leaf

July 8. I went and said my **Catechism** to-day. Came home and wrote down the questions and answers, then dressed and went to the dance, **endeavoured** to behave myself decent.

" 11. I improved my time before breakfast; after breakfast made some biscuits and did all my work before the sun was down.

" 12. I went to meeting and paid good attention to the sermon, came home and wrote down as much of it as I could remember.

" 17. I did everything before breakfast; endeavored to improve in school; went to the funeral in the afternoon, attended to what was said, came home and wrote down as much as I could remember.

" 25. A part of this day I **parsed** and endeavored to do well and a part of it I made some tarts and did some work and wrote a letter.

" 27. I did everything this morning same as usual, went to school and endeavored to be diligent; came home and **washed the butter** and assisted in getting coffee.

" 28. I endeavored to be diligent to-day in my learning, went from school to sit up with the sick, nursed her as well as I could.

" 30. I was pretty diligent at my work to-day and made a pudding for dinner.

Aug. 1. I got some peaches for to stew after I was done washing up the things and got my work and was **midlin** Diligent.

" 4. I did everything before breakfast and after breakfast got some peaches for Aunt Mell and then got my work and stuck pretty close to it and at night sat up with Sister and nursed her as good as I could.

" 8. I stuck pretty close to my work to-day and did all that Sister gave me and after I was done I swept out the house and put the things to rights.

" 9. I endeavored to improve my time to-day in reading and attending to what Brother read and most of the evening I was singing.

Religion and the alphabet were the only subjects taught in small colonial schools, called dame schools.

White Leaf: list of the duties Sumner performed

Catechism: summary of religious beliefs in question and answer form

endeavoured: (endeavored) tried hard

parsed: studied parts of speech

washed the butter: one of the steps in making butter from milk

midlin: (middling) fairly; average

1648 The four Puritan colonies of Massachusetts Bay, Plymouth, Connecticut, and New Haven form a council to plan church government.

1752 Puritans found the Midway Church in Georgia.

Colonial Sabbath Laws
by Joseph Bennett

Their: the Puritans'

pretence: (pretense) excuse

Lord's Day: Sabbath

town: Boston

fortification: fence

answer their end: serve the purpose; help the situation

offenders: wrongdoers

stopping up of highways: setting up blockades to prevent travel

tenacious: firm; holding onto ideas or principles

Common: land belonging to everyone

contiguous: next to

Moorfields, Finsbury: towns in England

disperse: scatter

liable to: likely to get

incurs: receives

Their observation of the sabbath . . . is the strictest kept that ever I yet saw anywhere. On that day, no man, woman, or child is permitted to go out of town on any **pretence** whatsoever; nor can any that are out of town come in on the **Lord's Day**. The **town** being situated on a peninsula, there is but one way out of it by land; which is over a narrow neck of land at the south end of the town, which is enclosed by a **fortification**, and the gates shut by way of prevention. There is a ferry, indeed, at the north end of the town; but care is taken by way of prevention there also. But, if they could escape out of the town at either of these places, it wouldn't **answer their end**: for the same care is taken, all the country over, to prevent travelling on Sundays; and they are as diligent in detecting of **offenders** of this sort, all over the New England Government, as we in England are of **stopping up of highways**. . . . And as they will by no means admit of trading on Sundays, so they are equally **tenacious** about preserving good order in the town on the Lord's Day; and they will not suffer any one to walk down to the water-side, though some of the houses are adjoining to the several wharfs; nor, even in the hottest days of summer, will they admit of any one to take the air on the **Common**, which lies **contiguous** to the town, as **Moorfields** does to **Finsbury**. And if two or three people, who meet one another in the street by accident, stand talking together,—if they do not **disperse** immediately upon the first notice, they are **liable to** fine and imprisonment; and I believe, whoever it be that **incurs** the penalties on this account, are sure to feel the weight

Puritans were not allowed to work on Sunday. Even food was prepared on Saturday so nothing would interfere with this day of worship.

of them. But that which is the most extraordinary is, that they **commence** the sabbath from the setting of the sun on the Saturday evening; and . . . all trade and business ceases, and every shop in the town is shut up: even a barber is **finable** for shaving after that time. Nor are any of the taverns permitted to entertain company; for, in that case, not only the house, but every person found therein, is finable. I don't mention this strict observation of the Lord's Day as intended rather to keep people within the bounds of decency and good order than to be strictly **complied with**, or that the appointment of this duty was only by some primary law since grown **obsolete**; but that it is now in full force and **vigor**, and that the **justices**, attended with a posse of **constables**, go about every week to **compel** obedience to this law.

commence: begin

finable: able to be fined

complied with: followed

obsolete: out-of-date

vigor: strength

justices: judges

constables: police officers

compel: force

Boston was a bustling colonial port city. For about two hundred years Boston was populated almost entirely by Puritans.

Mary Osgood Sumner was married at the age of 18 and widowed at 20. She and two of her sisters were lost at sea while traveling from Newport to New York. Her diary, which she called her "Monitor," was left behind. Joseph Bennett's studies detailed beliefs, laws, and the daily lives of the Puritans who settled in America.

From the diary of Mary Osgood Sumner in Alice Morse Earle's *Child Life in Colonial Days* (Williamstown, MA: Corner House Publishers, 1975), pp. 167–69. Reprinted by permission of the publisher. Colonial Sabbath Laws from Joseph Bennett, *History of New England* (Vol. V of *Proceedings of the Massachusetts Historical Society, 1860–1862*. Boston, 1862), pp. 115–16.

A Land of Opportunity?

" The sale of human beings in the market on board the ship is carried on. . . ."
Gottlieb Mittelberger

Female convicts were sometimes sent to the colonies as indentured servants. Those who married colonists had their contracts shortened.

Many Europeans signed contracts to pay for their passage to America. Known as indentured servants, they agreed to work for a certain number of years in return for their passage. Gottlieb Mittelberger, a German visiting Pennsylvania in the 1750s, describes life for indentured servants. Because some servants were mistreated, they ran away. Often the search for runaway servants was featured in newspaper ads.

security: something given or pledged as a guarantee

High-German: person who speaks the German language used in southern and central Germany

deem: think

When the ships have landed at Philadelphia after their long voyage, no one is permitted to leave them except those who pay for their passage or can give good **security**; the others, who cannot pay, must remain on board the ships till they are purchased, and are released from the ships by their purchasers. The sick always fare the worst, for the healthy are naturally preferred and purchased first; and so the sick and wretched must often remain on board in front of the city for 2 or 3 weeks, and frequently die, whereas many a one, if he could pay his debt and were permitted to leave the ship immediately, might recover and remain alive.

* * *

The sale of human beings in the market on board the ship is carried on thus: Every day Englishmen, Dutchmen and **High-German** people come from the city of Philadelphia and other places, in part from a great distance, say 20, 30, or 40 hours away, and go on board the newly arrived ship that has brought and offers for sale passengers from Europe, and select among the healthy persons such as they **deem** suitable for their business, and bargain with them how

1607

1607 First permanent English settlement is established in America.

1630 Over half of immigrants to America come as indentured servants.

long they will serve for their passage-money, which most of them are still in debt for. When they have come to an agreement, it happens that adult persons bind themselves in writing to serve 3, 4, 5 or 6 years for the amount due by them, according to their age and strength. But very young people, from 10 to 15 years, must serve till they are 21 years old.

Many parents must sell and trade away their children like so many head of cattle; for if their children take the debt upon themselves, the parents can leave the ship free and **unrestrained**; but as the parents often do not know where and to what people their children are going, it often happens that such parents and children, after leaving the ship, do not see each other again for many years, perhaps no more in all their lives.

When people arrive who cannot **make themselves free**, but have children under 5 years, the parents cannot free themselves by them; for such children must be given to somebody without **compensation** to be brought up, and they must serve for their bringing up till they are 21 years old. Children from 5 to 10 years, who pay half price for their passage, **viz.** 30 **florins**, must likewise serve for it till they are 21 years of age; they cannot, therefore, **redeem** their parents by taking the debt of the latter upon themselves. But children above 10 years can take part of their parents' debt upon themselves.

A woman must **stand for** her husband if he arrives sick, and in like manner a man for his sick wife, and take the debt upon herself or himself, and thus serve 5 to 6 years not alone for his or her own debt, but also for that of the sick husband or wife. But if both are sick, such persons are sent from the ship to the **sick-house**, but not until it appears probable that they will find no purchasers. As soon as they are well again they must serve for their passage, or pay if they have means.

It often happens that whole families, husband, wife, and children, are separated by being sold to different purchasers, especially when they have not paid any part of their passage money.

When a husband or wife has died at sea, when the ship has made more than half of her trip, the survivor must pay or serve not only for himself or herself, but also for the deceased.

Many Europeans found it hard to resist advertisements that glorified the benefits of living in the colonies.

unrestrained: not held back

make themselves free: pay their passage

compensation: payment

viz.: that is

florins: gold or silver coins used in some European countries

redeem: purchase the freedom of

stand for: represent

sick-house: hospital for the poor

1683 German immigrants settle in Germantown, Pennsylvania.

1750 By this year a million and a half people have settled in the thirteen colonies.

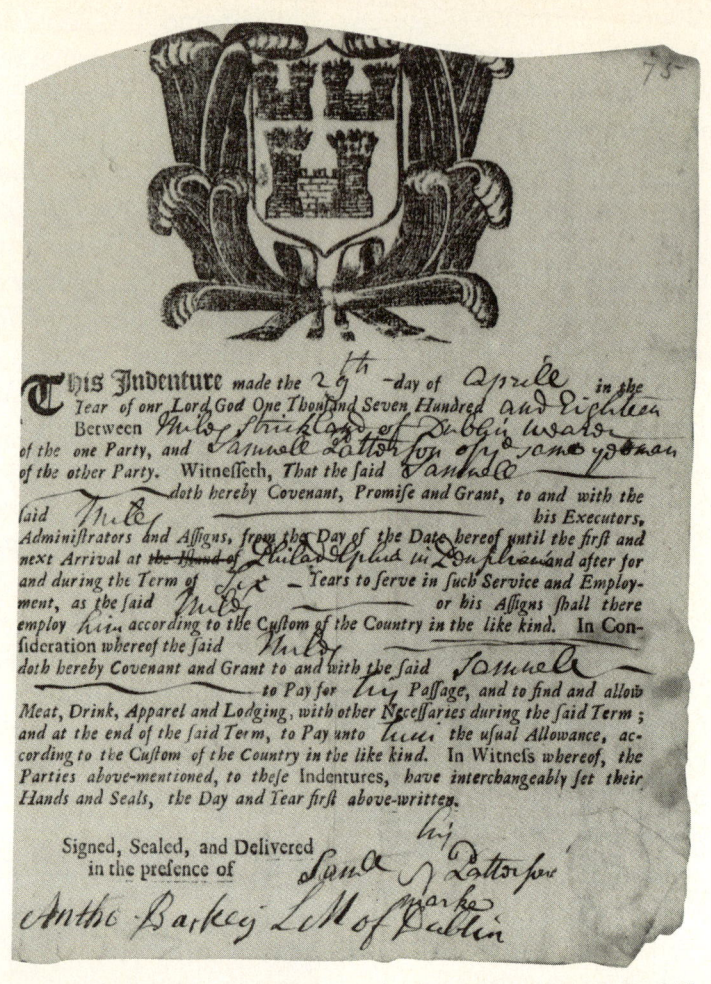

In this indenture, or contract, made in 1718, Samuel Patterson agrees to serve Miles Strickland for six years. In exchange Strickland agrees to pay for Patterson's voyage to America.

stipulated: agreed upon; demanded

serf: worker who is almost like a slave

pounds: British unit of money. One pound was equal to 240 pennies.

repented: felt sorry over something done and changed one's mind

exorbitantly: costly; expensive

ware: item that is bought

provision: arrangement

manifold: varied

When both parents have died over half-way at sea, their children, especially when they are young and have nothing to pawn or to pay, must stand for their own and their parents' passage, and serve till they are 21 years old. When one has served his or her term, he or she is entitled to a new suit of clothes at parting; and if it has been so **stipulated**, a man gets in addition a horse, a woman, a cow.

When a **serf** has an opportunity to marry in this country, he or she must pay for each year which he or she would have yet to serve, 5 to 6 **pounds**. But many a one who has thus purchased and paid for his bride, has subsequently **repented** his bargain, so that he would gladly have returned his **exorbitantly** dear **ware**, and lost the money besides.

If some one in this country runs away from his master, who has treated him harshly, he cannot get far. Good **provision** has been made for such cases, so that a runaway is soon recovered. He who detains or returns a deserter receives a good reward.

If such a runaway has been away from his master one day, he must serve for it as a punishment a week, for a week a month, and for a month half a year. But if the master will not keep the runaway after he has got him back, he may sell him for so many years as he would have to serve him yet.

Work and labor in this new and wild land are very hard and **manifold**, and many a one who came there in his old age must work very hard to his end for his bread. . . .

Ran away from his Master *Benjamin Bacon* of *Salem*, Wig-maker, *June* the 10th. his Apprentice Boy, *Samuel Dove*, aged 12 Years, who wears light coloured short Hair, having on when he went away, striped Jacket and Breeches, a check'd Shirt, and a Felt Hat. Whoever shall take up the abovesaid Runaway, and bring him to his said Master, shall have *Three Pounds*, **Old Tenor**, Reward, and all necessary Charges paid *per* me

Benjamin Bacon.

[From the *Boston Evening Post*, July 11, 1748]

Old Tenor: first paper money issued in Massachusetts

Germantown, July 18, 1759

Run away on the 13th of this Instant, at Night, from the Subscriber, of said Town, an Apprentice Lad, named Stophel, or Christopher Hergesheimer, about 19 Years of Age, by Trade a Blacksmith, middle sized of his Age, has a sour down-looking **Countenance**, is of Dutch **Extraction**, but can talk good English; Had on, and took with him, when he went away, a bluish **Cloath** Coat, green **Nap** Jacket, Snuff coloured Breeches, and Linen Jacket and Breeches, all about half wore, two pair of Ozenbrigs Trowsers, two **Ditto** Shirts, and one pretty fine, a Pair of old Shoes, a Pair of Thread, and a Pair of Cotton Stockings, a good **Athlone** Felt Hat, and yellowish Silk Handkerchief, wore his own dark brown short Hair, but may cut it off: He had a Hurt on the Inside of his Left-hand, not quite cured, at his going away. Whoever takes him up, and brings or **conveys** him to his Master, or secures him in the Jail of Philadelphia, shall have Forty **Shillings** Reward, and reasonable Charges, paid by

Matthew Potter, junior.

[From the *Pennsylvania Gazette*, August 2, 1759]

countenance: facial appearance

extraction: descent

cloath: (cloth)

nap: cloth with a fuzzy surface formed by very short fibers

ditto: similar; of the same kind

Athlone: style named for a county in Ireland

conveys: transfers; carries

shillings: silver coins of Great Britain. One shilling was equal to 12 pennies.

The life of the indentured servant was very hard. In some colonies masters had the right to beat or otherwise punish their servants for disobeying orders. Many of the runaway servants were originally convicts or victims of kidnapping forced into servitude against their will. Other servants signed contracts willingly and met the terms. They lived with their masters as members of the family and were successful once they gained their freedom.

From *America Before the Revolution 1725–1775*, edited by Alden T. Vaughan. Copyright © 1967. Used by permission of the publisher, Prentice-Hall, Inc., Englewood Cliffs, N.J.

UNIT 3

BIRTH OF A NATION

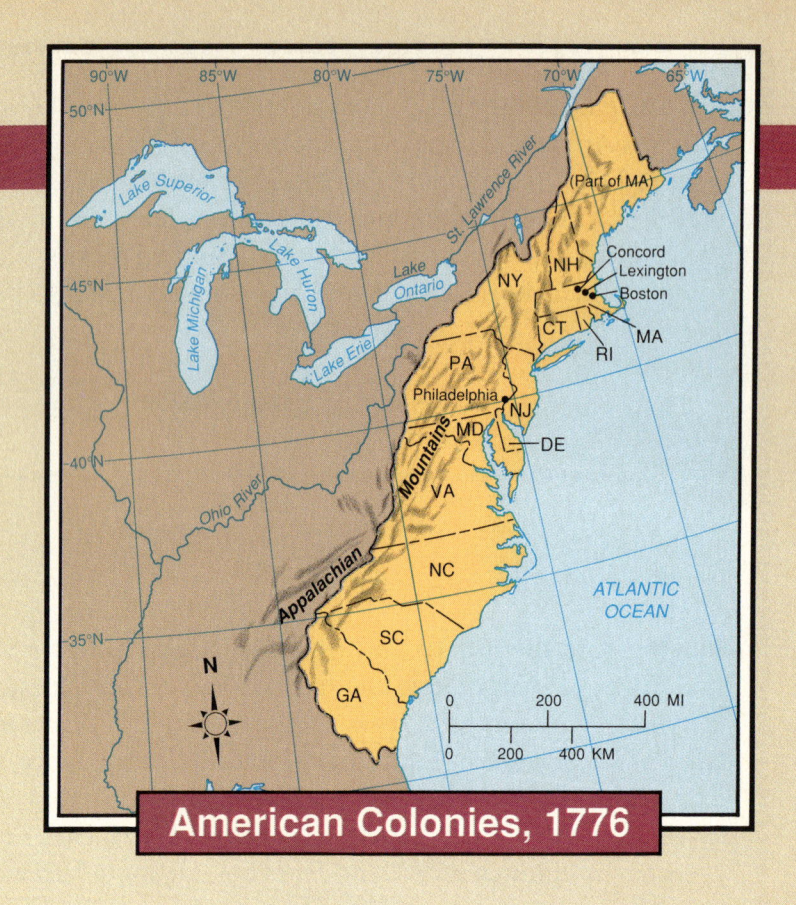

American Colonies, 1776

boycotting: refusing to buy

Intolerable Acts: laws that included closing Boston Harbor and forcing the colonists to house British troops in their homes

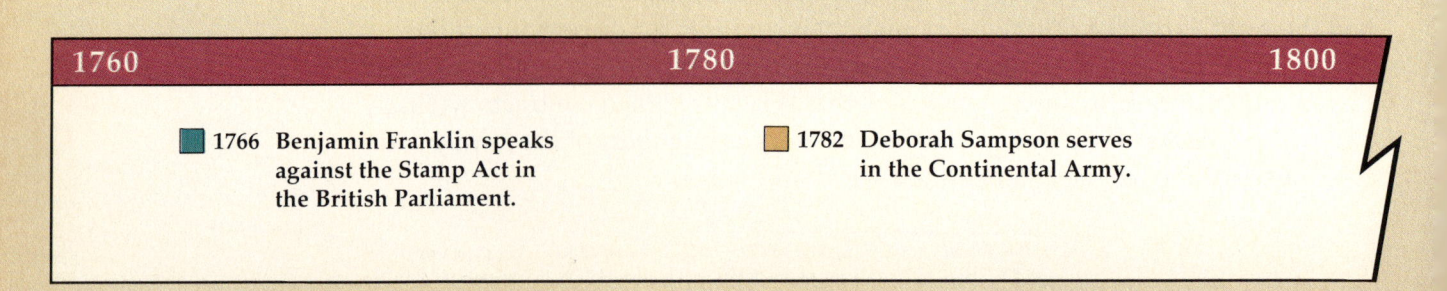

The American Revolution began long before the first shots were fired in 1775. As early as 1763 Great Britain began to enforce old trade laws that required the colonists to sell certain products only to Great Britain. Great Britain also increased the taxes that colonists were already paying on sugar and coffee. In 1765, however, the British levied a new tax on the colonists. The Stamp Act required a stamp to be purchased and placed on all printed materials, from newspapers to playing cards. The new tax outraged the colonists. "No taxation without representation!" they cried. The colonists protested the tax by **boycotting** many British goods and refusing to buy the stamps. The Stamp Act was repealed in 1766, but British-American relations were already damaged.

Great Britain continued to tax the colonists for everything from sugar to glass to tea. The colonists responded with further protests. Their violent outbursts, such as the Boston Massacre and the Boston Tea Party, angered the British. In 1774 the British enacted a series of harsh laws called the **Intolerable Acts** to punish the colonists. These laws spurred

---

1760 — 1780 — 1800

■ 1766 Benjamin Franklin speaks against the Stamp Act in the British Parliament.

■ 1782 Deborah Sampson serves in the Continental Army.

26

the colonists to action. War finally came on April 19, 1775, at Lexington and Concord in Massachusetts. The colonies raised an army and, in July 1776, declared their independence from Britain.

Poorly trained and equipped, the American army struggled for the first two years of the war. In 1777, however, the Americans soundly defeated a British force at Saratoga, New York. The victory convinced France to enter the war against the British. With French aid and the determination of General George Washington, the American army emerged victorious in 1783.

Thousands of Patriots contributed to the American victory. However, many years passed before blacks and women were fully able to enjoy the freedom they had helped win. But the spirit of the American Revolution lived on in them. A war for freedom had been fought and won.

General George Washington led colonists against the British in the Battle of Princeton in 1777. The colonists fought for eight years to win their independence from Great Britain.

This unit describes the roles of three people who contributed to the fight for independence.

- In testimony given before Parliament in 1766, **Benjamin Franklin** advises the British of the folly of the Stamp Act.
- **Deborah Sampson** describes being wounded in 1782 while disguised as a man serving in the Continental Army.
- **Jehu Grant**, a black soldier during the American Revolution, requests a pension for his service in the colonial army.

1820 **1840**

- 1836 Jehu Grant requests a soldier's pension for his service during the American Revolution.

A Taxing Problem

"In my opinion there is not gold and silver enough in the colonies to pay the stamp duty for one year."
Benjamin Franklin

Benjamin Franklin was called before the British Parliament to report on the colonists' reaction to the Stamp Act.

abode: residence

real and personal: property and money

excise: tax on certain goods

duty: tax on goods brought in from other countries

Negroes imported: slaves brought in from other countries

discharge: pay off

contracted: built up

ravaged: destroyed or ruined

impoverished: weakened

In 1765 the British Parliament passed the Stamp Act. American colonists had to pay taxes on all official papers. Immediately the colonists joined together to oppose this direct tax. Outraged at being taxed without having any representation, some colonists became violent. Others refused to buy anything made in England. In his testimony before Parliament in 1766, Benjamin Franklin explains why the Stamp Act is unwise.

Q. What is your name, and place of **abode?**
A. Franklin, of Philadelphia.
Q. Do the Americans pay any considerable taxes among themselves?
A. Certainly many, and very heavy taxes.
Q. What are the present taxes in Pennsylvania, laid by the laws of the colony?
A. There are taxes on all estates, **real and personal**; a poll tax; a tax on all offices, professions, trades, and businesses, according to their profits; an **excise** on all wine, rum, and other spirit; and a **duty** of ten pounds per head on all **Negroes imported**. . . .
Q. For what purposes are those taxes laid?
A. For the support of the civil and military establishments of the country, and to **discharge** the heavy debt **contracted** in the last war. . . .
Q. Are not all the people very able to pay those taxes?
A. No. The frontier counties, all along the continent, having been frequently **ravaged** by the enemy and greatly **impoverished**, are able to pay very little tax. . . .

1754		
1754 The French and Indian War begins.	**1763** British win the French and Indian War. Britain controls all of North America from the Atlantic Ocean to the Mississippi River.	**1765** The Stamp Act is passed by British Parliament. Riots erupt in America in response to the tax.

Q. Are not the colonies . . . very able to pay the stamp duty?
A. In my opinion there is not gold and silver enough in the colonies to pay the stamp duty for one year.
Q. Don't you know that the money arising from the stamps was all to be laid out in America?
A. I know it is **appropriated** by the act to the American service; but it will be spent in the **conquered colonies**, where the soldiers are, not in the colonies that pay it. . . .
Q. Do you think it right that America should be protected by this country and pay no part of the expense?
A. That is not the case. The colonies raised, clothed, and paid, during the last war, near 25,000 men, and spent many millions.

Q. Were you not **reimbursed** by Parliament?
A. We were only reimbursed what, in your opinion, we had advanced beyond our **proportion,** or beyond what might reasonably be expected from us; and it was a very small part of what we spent. Pennsylvania, in particular, **disbursed** about 500,000 pounds, and the reimbursements, in the whole, did not exceed 60,000 pounds. . . .
Q. Do not you think the people of America would submit to pay the stamp duty, if it was **moderated?**
A. No, never, unless **compelled** by **force of arms**. . . .
Q. What was the **temper** of America towards Great Britain before the year 1763?

appropriated: assigned

conquered colonies: French Canada and other areas that the French had controlled

reimbursed: paid back

proportion: fair share

disbursed: paid out

moderated: made less costly

compelled: forced

force of arms: the military

temper: mood; feeling

Groups of protestors who called themselves the "Sons of Liberty" met in towns throughout the colonies in an effort to have the Stamp Act repealed.

| 1766 | Franklin testifies before Parliament. The Stamp Act is repealed. | 1767 | Parliament passes Townshend Acts, placing new duties on Americans. | 1768 | British troops arrive in Boston to keep law and order. | 1770 | Five colonists are killed by British soldiers in the Boston Massacre. |

resolutions: formal statements

this House: the House of Commons, the branch of Parliament to which common people are elected

House of Lords: the branch of Parliament made up of members of the upper class

repealed: removed; voted out of law

A. The best in the world. They submitted willingly to the government of the Crown, and paid, in all their courts, obedience to acts of Parliament. . . .
Q. What is your opinion of a future tax, imposed on the same principle with that of the Stamp Act? How would the Americans receive it?
A. Just as they do this. They would not pay it.
Q. Have not you heard of the **resolutions** of **this House**, and of the **House of Lords,** asserting the right of Parliament relating to America, including a power to tax the people there?
A. Yes, I have heard of such resolutions.
Q. What will be the opinion of the Americans on those resolutions?
A. They will think them unconstitutional and unjust.
Q. Was it an opinion in America before 1763 that the Parliament had no right to lay taxes and duties there?
A. I never heard any objection to the right of laying duties to regulate commerce; but a right to lay internal taxes was never supposed to be in Parliament, as we are not represented there. . . .
Q. Did the Americans ever dispute the controlling power of Parliament to regulate the commerce?
A. No.
Q. Can anything less than a military force carry the Stamp Act into execution?
A. I do not see how a military force can be applied to that purpose.
Q. Why may it not?
A. Suppose a military force sent into America; they will find nobody in arms; what are they then to do? They cannot force a man to take stamps who chooses to do without them. They will not find a rebellion; they may indeed make one.
Q. If the act is not **repealed,** what do you think will be the consequences?
A. A total loss of the respect and affection the people of America bear to this country, and of all the commerce that depends on that respect and affection.

Stamps appeared on deeds, licenses, almanacs, newspapers, and even dice and playing cards to indicate that the tax had been paid on those items.

Angry mobs of protestors seized stamps and stamp paper from the tax offices and burned them in the streets.

Q. How can the commerce be affected?
A. You will find that, if the act is not repealed, they will take very little of your **manufactures** in a short time.
Q. Is it in their power to do without them?
A. I think they may very well do without them.
Q. Is it their interest not to take them?
A. The goods they take from Britain are either necessaries, mere conveniences, or **superfluities.** The first, as cloth, etc., with a little industry they can make at home; the second they can do without till they are able to provide them among themselves; and the last, which are much the greatest part, they will **strike off** immediately. They are mere articles of fashion, purchased and consumed because the fashion in a respected country; but will now be detested and rejected. The people have already struck off, by general agreement, the use of all goods fashionable in mournings. . . .
Q. If the Stamp Act should be repealed, would it **induce** the **assemblies** of America to acknowledge the right of Parliament to tax them, and would they erase their resolutions?
A. No, never.
Q. Is there no means of **obliging** them to erase those resolutions?
A. None that I know of; they will never do it, unless compelled by force of arms.
Q. Is there a power on earth that can force them to erase them?
A. No power, how great soever, can force men to change their opinions. . . .
Q. What used to be the pride of the Americans?
A. To indulge in the fashions and manufactures of Great Britain.
Q. What is now their pride?
A. To wear their old clothes over again, till they can make new ones.

manufactures: goods or products

superfluities: goods that are not needed

strike off: stop buying

induce: make

assemblies: legislatures

obliging: getting

Franklin testified in February 1766. The Stamp Act was repealed in March. The British, however, soon found other ways to tax the colonies. In 1767 the Townshend Acts taxed certain imported British goods. Colonists reacted even more violently than before. In answer to this violence British soldiers were sent to the colonies. The foundation of the American Revolution had been laid.

From *The Parliamentary History of England, 1066–1803,* (reprint ed., New York: AMS Press, 1966).

Wounded in Action

"But I had less dread of receiving half a dozen more balls than the penetrating glance of his eye."

Deborah Sampson

Deborah Sampson disguised herself as a man to fight in the Revolutionary War.

The idea of going to war appealed to Deborah Sampson's sense of adventure. So in 1782 she dressed as a man and enlisted in the colonial army. She was wounded that same year in combat. In this account she describes her fear of having her true identity discovered while being treated for the wound. This story, based on her memories, was written years later by her and Herman Mann.

I considered this as a death wound, or as being equivalent to it; as it must, I thought, lead to the discovery of my sex. Covered with blood from head to foot, I told my companions I fear I had received a **mortal** wound; and I begged them to leave me to die on the spot: preferring to take the small chance I should in this case have of surviving, rather than to be carried to the hospital. To this my comrades would not consent; but one of them took me before him on his horse, and in this painful manner I was **borne** six miles to the hospital of the French army. . . .

The French surgeon, on my being brought in, instantly came. He was alert, cheerful, **humane**. "How you lose so much blood at this early hour? Be any bone broken?" was his first salutation. . . . My head having been bound up, and a change of clothing becoming a wounded soldier being ready, I was asked by the too inquisitive French surgeon whether I had any other wound. He had observed my extreme paleness, and that I limped in attempting to walk. I readily replied in the negative: it was a plump falsehood! "Sit you down my lad; your boot say you fib!" said

mortal: fatal

borne: carried

humane: kind

1775

1775 The American Revolution begins.

the surgeon, noticing that the blood still oozed from it. He took off my boots and stockings . . . and washed my leg to the knee. I then told him I would retire, change my clothing, and if any other wound should appear, I would inform him.

Meanwhile I had **procured** in the hospital a silver **probe** a little curved at the end, a needle, some **lint**, a bandage, and some of the same kind of salve that had been applied to the wound in my head. I found that the **ball** had penetrated my thigh about two inches, and the wound was still moderately bleeding. . . . At the third attempt I **extracted** the ball.

This operation over . . . I was again visited by the surgeon. In his watchful eye I plainly read doubts. I told him that all was well; that I felt much **revived,** and wished to sleep. I had slept scarcely an hour, when he again alarmed me. Approaching me on my mattress of straw, and holding my breeches in his hand, dripping from the washtub, "How came this **rent**?" said he, putting his finger into it. I replied, "It was occasioned, I believe, on horseback, by a nail in the saddle or holster. 'Tis of no consequence. Sleep refreshes me. I had none last night." One half of this, certainly, was true. But I had less dread of receiving half a dozen more balls than the penetrating glance of his eye. As I grew better his **scrutiny** diminished.

procured: acquired or gotten

probe: surgical instrument

lint: gauze

ball: bullet

extracted: removed

revived: healthier; in a better condition

rent: tear

scrutiny: long, careful looks

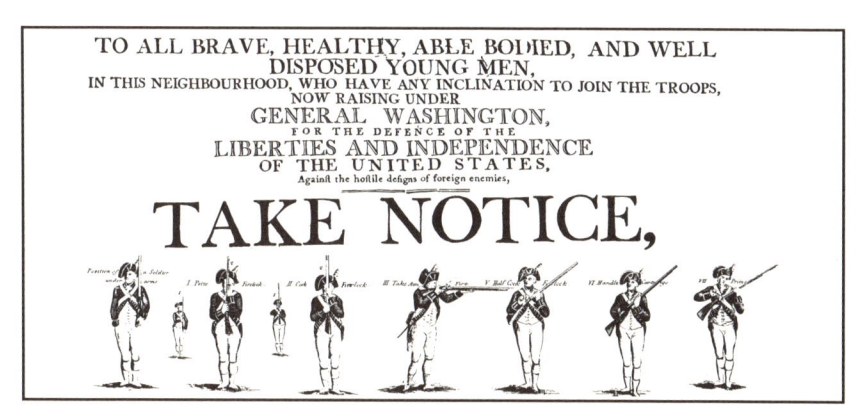

This poster urged men to enlist in the newly formed Continental Army. When Washington rode into Massachusetts, 15,000 new soldiers awaited him.

Sampson recovered from her wound. Her true identity was eventually discovered, but she served in the army until October 1783. She worked for a while on her uncle's farm. There she met and married Benjamin Gannett. In 1792 she asked Congress to give her pay she had not received while in the army. Later she received a pension for being wounded in the service of her country. She died in 1827.

From *The Female Review: Life of Deborah Sampson,* ed. Herman Mann (New York: Arno Press, 1972), pp. 168–69.

1782 Disguised as a man, Deborah Sampson enlists in the Continental Army. She is wounded in combat.

1783 The American Revolution ends. Sampson is honorably discharged from the army.

1783

33

Colonial Soldier

"These considerations induced me to enlist into the American army, where I served faithful about ten months. . . ."

Jehu Grant

When the Revolutionary War began, only free blacks were allowed to enlist in the army. Later, slaves were also allowed to join.

At the time of the American Revolution about one fifth of the people in the colonies were black. Most of these were slaves. The idea of freedom for which the colonists fought was appealing to these slaves. About 5,000 black men served in the Continental Army. Years later some of these black soldiers applied for pensions from the government. In this letter Jehu Grant asks again for the pension he feels he earned.

leave: permission

arbitrary: unfair

liberty poles: flagpoles with symbols of liberty on them

> *Hon. J. L. Edwards, Commissioner of Pensions:*
> Your servant begs **leave** to state that he forwarded to the War Department a declaration founded on the Pension Act of June 1832 praying to be allowed a pension (if his memory serves him) for ten months' service in the American army of the Revolutionary War. . . .
>
> I was then grown to manhood, in the full vigor and strength of life, and heard much about the cruel and **arbitrary** things done by the British. Their ships lay within a few miles of my master's house, which stood near the shore, and I was confident that my master traded with them, and I suffered much from fear that I should be sent aboard a ship of war. This I disliked. But when I saw **liberty poles** and the people all engaged for the support of freedom, I could not but like and be pleased with such thing. . . . And living on the borders of Rhode Island, where whole companies of colored people enlisted, it added to my fears and dread of

1775

- **1775** Battles of Lexington and Concord begin the American Revolution.
- **1777** Jehu Grant joins the army of Rhode Island.
- **1783** The Treaty of Paris is signed. The American Revolution ends.

being sold to the British. These considerations **induced** me to enlist into the American army, where I served faithful about ten months, when my master found and took me home. Had I been taught to read or understand the **precepts of the Gospel**, "Servants obey your masters," I might have done otherwise, notwithstanding the songs of liberty that saluted my ear, thrilled through my heart. But feeling conscious that I have since **compensated** my master for the **injury he sustained** by my enlisting, and that God has forgiven me for so doing, and that I served my country faithfully, and that they having enjoyed the benefits of my service to an equal degree for the length [of] time I served with those generally who are receiving the **liberalities** of the government, I cannot but feel it becoming me to pray Your Honor to review my declaration on file and the papers **herewith** amended.

A few years after the war, Joshua Swan, **Esq.**, of Stonington purchased me of my master and agreed that after I had served him a length of time named faithfully, I should be free. I served to his satisfaction and so obtained my freedom. . . . After my time expired with Esq. Swan, I married a wife. We have raised six children. Five are still living. I must be upward of eighty years of age and have been blind for many years, and, notwithstanding the aid I received from the honest industry of my children, we are still very needy and in part are supported from the **benevolence** of our friends. With these statements and the testimony of my character herewith presented, I humbly set my claim upon the well-known liberality of government.

Most respectfully your humble servant

Jehu ✠ Grant
his mark

---

induced: caused

precepts of the Gospel: sayings of the Bible

compensated: paid back

injury he sustained: the work time he lost

liberalities: money; pensions

herewith: with this; attached

Esq.: (Esquire) title of respect

benevolence: charity

Unfortunately, Jehu Grant was never granted his pension. Although he had served faithfully in the American army, he did so while he was a fugitive slave. This, according to the government, made him ineligible for a pension. However, the great contribution made by black Americans to the cause of freedom cannot be forgotten. Their efforts played an important role in shaping the history of the United States.

From *The Revolution Remembered*, ed. John C. Dann (Chicago: The University of Chicago Press, 1980), pp. 27–28. Copyright © 1980 by The University of Chicago.

1832 Jehu Grant applies for a veteran's pension but is denied.

1836 Jehu Grant applies for a veteran's pension again and is denied a second time.

UNIT 4

ON THE MOVE

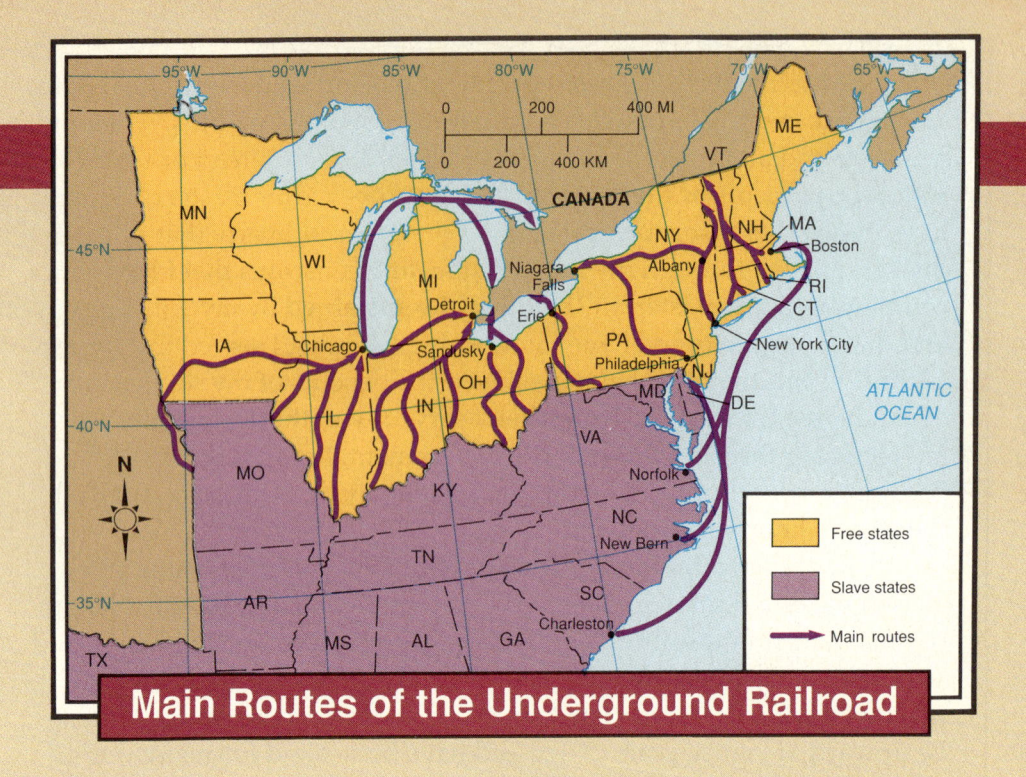

Main Routes of the Underground Railroad

cholera: an often fatal epidemic disease that causes cramps, nausea, vomiting, and dehydration

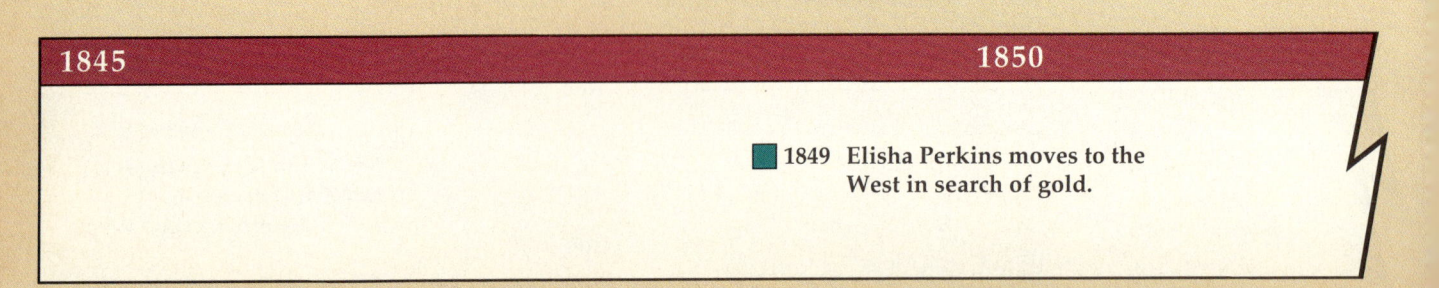

A fierce desire for freedom combined with a boldness of spirit had made the colonists victorious in the American Revolution. This same spirit helped to push Americans west to explore and settle new lands. At the end of the American Revolution the boundary of the United States reached westward only to the Mississippi River. Fourteen states belonged to the Union. But less than a century later 32 states belonged to a united nation that stretched from coast to coast.

"Westward, ho!" became the cry of hundreds of thousands of settlers, eager to stake their claims on the seemingly limitless, fertile land in the West. Millions of immigrants poured into America, and the population of the United States soared. Immigrants and Americans alike streamed westward in search of new beginnings. By 1820 almost 800,000 settlers had crossed the Appalachian Mountains. By 1860 they had passed through the Great Plains.

Pioneers struggled through months of monotonous travel, carrying all their belongings in covered wagons. They crossed mountains and rivers, and endured scorching heat and torrential rains. **Cholera** epidemics raged up and down the westbound trails, claiming thousands of lives. Many other pioneers died in accidents. Settlers also disputed with Native

1845	1850
	■ 1849 Elisha Perkins moves to the West in search of gold.

Americans over land. Thousands of Native Americans died in battle. Many also died from diseases brought by settlers.

Land was not the only attraction in the West. Late in 1848 gold was discovered in a mill stream in California. People rushed to California, dreaming of striking it rich. Most gold miners found backbreaking work and only enough gold to pay their expenses. In less than two years California's population swelled from about 15,000 to more than 100,000.

Meanwhile the plantations of the South continued to rely on slavery. In the 1830s free blacks, **Quakers,** and other white **abolitionists** defied the strict fugitive slave laws. These groups developed the Underground Railroad, a network of people, called "conductors," and places, or "stations," created to move slaves secretly to safety in the free states and Canada.

Quakers: religious group noted for their efforts in education and beliefs in nonviolence and racial equality

abolitionists: people who favored the abolition or end of slavery in the United States

Thousands of people flooded to the West in the 1800s. Deep ruts cut by wagon wheels can still be found on some of the heavily traveled trails.

This unit contains the stories of three people involved in the changes and challenges of the expanding United States.

- In his diary **Elisha Perkins** describes the excitement and hardships of mining California gold.
- **Amelia Stewart Knight** recounts in her diary the daily life of a pioneer family on the long Oregon Trail.
- **William Still** describes the successful but dangerous escape from slavery by **William "Box" Peel Jones**.

1855   1860

- 1853 Amelia Stewart Knight travels westward on the Oregon Trail, along with thousands of other settlers.
- 1859 William "Box" Peel Jones escapes from slavery through the Underground Railroad.

Gold Rush Diary

❝ Tis terrible hard work, & such a backache as we have every night! ❞
Elisha Douglass Perkins

As word spread that gold had been discovered in California, thousands of Americans set off for the West to find their fortune.

found wanting: is not as good as hoped

Sac. City: Sacramento, California

&c: (et cetera) and so on

washers: pans used for separating gold from gravel

under the weather: not feeling well; ill

adz: axelike tool with a curved blade

"ripples" dash screen: part of the washer used to catch the gold

commence: begin

When gold was discovered in California in 1848, the news traveled quickly to the East. In 1849 more than 80,000 people, known as forty-niners, went west in search of gold. Many of them followed a trail mapped earlier by army surveyor John Frémont. Some were lucky, for there was gold, but most found just enough to keep them going. In his diary Elisha Perkins tells about the difficult and disappointing life of a prospector.

November 1.

Well here we are in the gold mines of California, & mining has been tried "& **found wanting**!" We left **Sac. City** October 18, with our provisions **&c** in Chapins wagons en route for the Cosumne River distant some 28 or 30 miles & arrived here the 21. We are about S.E. from the city, in a rolling country & on a small rapid stream tumbling over a rocky bed. The appearance of the country through which we passed was somewhat better than that down the Sac. River, as we saw it, but yet I have not been in any part of the "beautiful valley" of which we used to hear. On locating here we immediately went to work making **"washers."** Doc & John being somewhat "**under the weather**" I did nearly all the work on the mine alone. I cut down a pine tree, cut it off the proper length peeled & cut down one side & with axe & **adz** hollowed it out till I reduced it to about $\frac{1}{2}$ inch in thickness by nearly two days of hard labor & blistering of hands &c, & another day put in the **"ripples" dash screen** &c & took it down to the rocky bar where we are to **commence** our fortunes! & since have worked away like a

1848

| 1848 Discovery of gold at Sutter's Mill in California sparks the Gold Rush. | 1849 Thousands of prospectors go to California seeking gold. | 1850 California becomes a state. |

trooper, rain or shine, with but **indifferent** success.

The first three days Doc took hold with pick & shovel we **excavated** a hole about 4 feet deep & made in that time about **2.00**! Here Doc broke down & was taken sick & John being about **recruited** he commenced with me in another place & we have made something everyday, the highest **11.00** lowest **3** each. This wont do & we shall probably leave soon for richer **diggings** next week. Tis terrible hard work, & such a backache as we have every night! We are below the bed of the creek & have to bale out water from our "hole" every hour, & work in the mud & wet at its bottom. . . .

Thursday Nov.

Still in our camp on the Consumne & poor as the "diggings" have proved are likely to remain here all winter. The rains have set in in **earnest** & teams cannot travel. Chapins teams went to town for our provisions & **sundries** & are stuck fast about 5 miles from here, not able to move a step. I fear we may have difficulty in getting anything to eat. Doc has finally left us for good, & will probably go home in the next steamer, couldn't stand the hard work & went to town last week. His leaving puts the finishing stroke to my list of disappointments "& now I'm all alone." Shall have to give up my expectations of **accumulating sufficient** to carry me home in the spring & be thankful if I get enough to pay my expenses this winter. Well I'm here & must take the country as I find it. . . .

Christmas Day, 1849.

Oh how I wish I could spend this day at home, what a "merry Christmas" I would have of it, & what happy faces I should see

indifferent: neither good nor bad

excavated: dug

2.00, 11.00, 3: $2.00, $11.00, $3.00

recruited: restored to health

diggings: places to dig for gold

earnest: full force

sundries: various items

accumulating sufficient: getting enough money

Miners lined the banks of streams during the Gold Rush. Many used large metal pans with sloping sides to sift through the gravel for gold.

1852 $81 million worth of gold is found during this peak year of the Gold Rush.

1860 The great Gold Rush ends.

ushered: brought

lieu: place

Sierra Nevada: mountain range 400 miles long in eastern California

prevailing: most common

monotonous: dull; boring

dwindle down: grow smaller

mill race: the fast-moving stream of water that causes a mill wheel to turn

superintendants: (superintendents) managers; bosses

instead of these of the disappointed set now around me. The day here **ushered** in by firing of guns pistols &c & some blasting of heavy logs in **lieu** of cannon & this is about the amount of our celebrating. . . .

We are now situated about 50 miles from the **Sierra Nevada**, about 5 from the McCosme & near a famous diggings called "Matheney's Creek" or "Dead Man's Hollow," from a couple of men having been murdered here for their gold this past summer. . . .

Shortly after our arrival we were greeted in our new home in these higher altitudes by a heavy fall of snow & as we found our light clothes rather uncomfortable, John & myself went to work immediately building a cabin & after a week or ten days hard labor succeeded in erecting a very snug neat little house about 7 x 9 inside. & having most everything in are now comfortably installed—a good fire blazing in our own stone fireplace, & are sitting by it congratulating ourselves that we are not

Few prospectors struck it rich during the Gold Rush. Some found small nuggets worth only a few dollars—barely enough for food and supplies.

exposed to the cold rainy weather which is now **prevailing**. As yet we have had no opportunity to try the diggings here, between the unpleasant weather & our building, our time has all been taken up. We are encamped on a small creek running north. "Matheney's" famous hollow is just over a ridge east of us but has too much water to be worked this winter. We shall probably try it in the spring. Our life is **monotonous** enough. We have to amuse ourselves the best way we can by reading over & over the few books we have, playing cards, smoking &c. . . .

Saturday Feb 28.

Have just returned from an expedition round the richest of the mines of which we have heard to see about our summers digging, & find however that all the rich accounts **dwindle down** as you approach their location into the success of some few lucky ones & am satisfied by my trip that the gold is pretty equally distributed through the country, & a man had better settle down somewhere & work steadily for what he can get & trust to chance for striking a rich hole.

I went through Weaverton, Hangtown, Georgetown, where the Oregon men did so well & came back by way of Colloma & Sutter's Mill & stopped to see the famous place where the first discovery was made—the news of which had set the American world crazy. The mill stands on the American river, is surrounded by immense & almost perpendicular hills, & the discovery of gold was made in the **mill race** some hundred or more yards below the mill. The race was dug by Indians employed by Sutter with white **superintendants** over them. One of the Indians in excavating picked up a lump of something yellow—metallic & heavy which was examined by the superintendant & finally taken to Mrs. Weimar wife of one of the white men. This lady boiled the lump in strong **lye** for two hours without tarnishing it at all. It was then sent to San Francisco analyzed & examined & pronounced to be fine gold & hence spread the news like wild fire which has filled the wilderness of California with **enterprising** Yankees.

The spring seems to have at last set in with beautiful weather & we are beginning to think of moving & shall probably move over into Matheney's Creek next week. We have had two heavy falls of snow since December & the tops of the high hills are still covered. One snow fell over two feet deep.

From the top of a peak $\frac{1}{2}$ of a mile back of our cabin can be seen the Sierra Nevada range, white as snow itself, completely covered, shrubbery & all, distant from 30 to 50 miles East. While westward can be seen the valley of the Sacramento, with its boundary ranges of Cascade Mountains on the Pacific & the bay & entrance to San Francisco distant about 140 miles & the eye can follow the valley N.W. up some 200 miles. The view is Extensive & magnificent. During the late pleasant weather John & myself have been working in some of the little ravines & have made something over 100 dollars—better than nothing, though small wages.

lye: chemical from wood ashes used in making soap

enterprising: bold; ambitious

When one person discovered gold, hundreds more would flock to the area. Boom towns like Columbia, California, sprang up overnight. Many townspeople made their living by setting up businesses such as supply stores, barbershops, and hotels.

Elisha Perkins continued to prospect for gold but did not strike it rich. In 1851 he gave up and became a steamboat captain, piloting a steamer which carried cargo on the Sacramento River. After his death in 1852 the journal Perkins had kept as a miner was given to his wife. It was badly stained and blurred, but his wife made an exact copy of it to preserve it. This copy is the source of the reading.

From *Gold Rush Diary*, ed. Thomas D. Clark (Lexington: University of Kentucky Press, 1967), pp. 147, 149–51, 153–54. Reprinted by permission of the publisher.

Diary of an Oregon Pioneer

" We are not alone on these bare plains, it is covered with cattle and wagons...."
Amelia Stewart Knight

Between 1840 and 1870 covered wagons dotted the Great Plains. People were eager to claim the free land in the West.

In 1848 the Oregon Territory on the Pacific Coast officially became part of the United States. Thousands of people moved west. Most of them organized wagon trains in Missouri to travel the nearly 2,000 miles over prairies, deserts, and mountains to the Pacific Northwest. Because it was such a dangerous and difficult trip, pioneers could travel only about 20 miles a day. In her diary Amelia Knight tells what life was like on the Oregon Trail.

Saturday, April 9, 1853
Started from home about 11 o'clock and traveled 8 miles and camped in an old house: night cold and frosty.

Thursday, April 21st
Rained all night; is still raining. I have just counted 17 wagons traveling ahead of us in the mud and water. No feed for our poor stock to be got at any price. Have to feed them flour and meal. Traveled 22 miles today.

Tuesday, April 26th
Cold and clear; found corn last night at 2 dollars a bushel. Paid 12 dollars for about half a feed for our stock. I can count twenty wagons winding up the hill ahead of us. Traveled 20 miles and camp.

Friday, April 29th
Cool and pleasant; saw the first Indians today. Lucy and Almira afraid and run into the wagon to hide. Done some washing and sewing.

1805

1805 Lewis and Clark explore the territory from Missouri to the Pacific Ocean.

1841 Pioneers begin following the trail to Oregon.

1842 John C. Frémont surveys part of the Oregon Trail.

Monday, May 2nd

Pleasant evening; have been cooking, and packing things away for an early start in the morning. Threw away several jars, some wooden buckets, and all our pickles. Too unhandy to carry. Indians came to our camp every day, begging money and something to eat. Children are getting used to them.

Friday, May 6th

. . . Here we passed a train of wagons on their way back, the head man had been drowned a few days before, in a river called **Elkhorn**, while getting some cattle across and his wife was lying in the wagon quite sick, and children were mourning for the father gone. With sadness and pity I passed those who perhaps a few days before had been well and happy as ourselves. Came 20 miles today.

Sunday, May 8th

Still in camp. Waiting to cross [the Elkhorn River]. There are three hundred or more wagons in sight and as far as the eye can reach, the bottom is covered, on each side of the river, with cattle and horses. There is no ferry here and the men will have to make one out of the tightest wagon-bed (every company should have a waterproof wagon-bed for this purpose.) Everything must now be hauled out of the wagons **head over heels** (and he who knows where to find anything will be a smart fellow.) then the wagons must be all taken to pieces, and then by means of a strong rope stretched across the river with a tight wagon-bed attached to the middle of it, the rope must be long enough to pull from one side to the other, with men on each side of the river to pull it. In this way we have to cross everything a little at a time. Women and children last, and then swim the cattle and horses. There were three horses and some cattle drowned while crossing this place yesterday. It is quite lively and merry here this morning and the weather fine. We are camped on a large bottom, with the broad, deep river on one side of us and a high bluff on the other.

Monday, May 16th

Evening—We have had all kinds of weather today. This morning was dry, dusty and sandy. This afternoon it rained, hailed, and the wind was very high. Have been traveling all the afternoon in mud and water up to our hubs. Broke chains and stuck

Elkhorn: river in northeastern Nebraska

head over heels: in a hurry and in no order

Once the new settlers picked out a parcel of land, they began building houses using logs from nearby forests.

1843 The first large group of settlers—about 1,000—takes the Oregon Trail west.

1848 Oregon becomes a territory.

1859 Oregon becomes a state.

Covered wagons were loaded down with household goods, food, and wagon parts for repairs. Those who overpacked often had to toss out some of their belongings along the trail.

lighting: (lightning)

commenced: began

brute: animal

that: (than)

prospect: view; sight

droves: herds; groups

fool of a job: easy work

drovers: herders; cowhands

lawless set: rough, threatening drovers

teamster: person who drives a team

hollowing: (hollering)

in the mud several times. The men and boys are all wet and muddy. Hard times but they say misery loves company. We are not alone on these bare plains, it is covered with cattle and wagons. . . .

Tuesday, May 17th

We had a dreadful storm of rain and hail last night and very sharp **lighting**. It killed two oxen for one man. We have just encamped on a large flat prairie, when the storm **commenced** in all its fury and in two minutes after the cattle were taken from the wagons every **brute** was gone out of sight, cows, calves, horses, all gone before the storm like so many wild beasts. I never saw such a storm. The wind was so high I thought it would tear the wagons to pieces. Nothing but the stoutest covers could stand it. The rain beat into the wagons so that everything was wet, in less **that** 2 hours the water was a foot deep all over our camp grounds. As we could have no tents pitched, all had to crowd into the wagons and sleep in wet beds with their wet clothes on, without supper. The wind blew hard all night and this morning presents a dreary **prospect** surrounded by water, and our saddles have been soaking in it all night and are almost spoiled! . . .

Tuesday, May 31st

Evening—Traveled 25 miles today. When we started this morning there were two large **droves** of cattle and about 50 wagons ahead of us, and we either had to stay poking behind them in the dust or hurry up and drive past them. It was no **fool of a job** to be mixed up with several hundred head of cattle, and only one road to travel in, and the **drovers** threatening to drive their cattle over you if you attempted to pass them. They even took out their pistols. Husband came up just as one man held his pistol at Wilson Carl and saw what the fuss was and said, "Boys, follow me," and he drove our team out of the road entirely, and the cattle seemed to understand it all, for they went into the trot most of the way. The rest of the boys followed with their teams and the rest of the stock. I had rather a rough ride to be sure, but was glad to get away from such **lawless set**, which we did by noon. The head **teamster** done his best by whipping and **hollowing** to his cattle. He found it no use and got up into his wagon to take it easy. We left some swearing men behind us. We drove a good ways ahead and stopped to rest the cattle and eat some dinner. While we were eating we saw them coming. All hands jumped for their teams saying they had earned the road too dearly to let them pass us again, and in a few moments we were all on the go again. Had been very warm today. Thermometer at 98 in the wagon at one o'clock. Towards evening there came up a light thunderstorm which cooled the air down to 60. We are now within 100 miles of **Fort Laramie**.

Wednesday, June 1st

It has been raining all day long and we have been traveling in it so as to be able to keep ahead of the large droves. The men and boys are all soaking wet and look sad and comfortless. (The little ones and myself are shut up in the wagons from the rain. Still it will find its way in and many things are wet; and take us all together we are a poor looking set, and all this for Oregon. I am thinking while I write, "Oh, Oregon, you must be a wonderful country." Came 18 miles today.)

Fort Laramie: army fort in eastern Wyoming near the Nebraska border

At night wagon trains formed a large circle that served as a corral for livestock and a defense against attacks by Native Americans.

Like other pioneers the Knight family overcame many problems during their five-month journey west. In September as the wagons came into Oregon, Amelia delivered the family's eighth child. With the new baby the family crossed the Columbia River by canoe and flatboat, traded oxen for a piece of land and a log cabin, and began a new life in the Oregon Territory.

Excerpt from Amelia Stewart Knight, "Diary of an Oregon Pioneer of 1853." *Transactions of the Oregon Pioneer Association* (Portland: Oregon Historical Society, 1928), pp. 38–56.

Wrapped in Straw and Boxed Up

" He . . . felt that no man was safe while owned by another."

William Still

It is estimated that by the 1850s more than 1,000 slaves were escaping from their owners each year.

admonished: warned

liable: likely

market: place in which slaves were sold

not admitting of straightening himself out: not having room to extend his legs or back

taxed: tested

verge: point

ere: before

During the years slavery existed in the United States, thousands of slaves escaped to the North. They were often helped along a secret route called the Underground Railroad. William Still, leader of Philadelphia's Underground Railroad, describes the dangerous escape of a slave, William Peel Jones. A letter written for Jones addressed to Still contains many spelling errors. Many people of the time had little education.

William is twenty-five years of age, unmistakably colored, good-looking, rather under the medium size, and of pleasing manners. William had himself boxed up by a near relative and forwarded by the Erricson line of steamers. He gave the slip to Robert H. Carr, his owner (a grocer and commission merchant), . . . for the following reasons: For some time previous his master had been selling off his slaves every now and then, the same as other groceries, and this **admonished** William that he was **liable** to be in the **market** any day; consequently, he preferred the box to the auction-block.

He did not complain of having been treated very badly by Carr, but felt that no man was safe while owned by another. In fact, he "hated the very name of slaveholder." The limit of the box **not admitting of straightening himself out** he was taken with the cramp on the road, suffered indescribable misery, and had his faith **taxed** to the utmost—indeed was brought to the very **verge** of "screaming aloud" **ere** relief came. However, he controlled himself,

1815		
1815 System to aid escaped slaves is operating regularly in Ohio.	**1820** Most Northern states abolish slavery; antislavery groups grow stronger.	**1830** The term "Underground Railroad" is first used.

though only for a short **season**, for before a great while an excessive faintness came over him. Here nature became quite exhausted. He thought he must "die"; but his time had not yet come. After a severe struggle he **revived**, but only to encounter a third **ordeal** no less painful than the one through which he had just passed. Next a very "cold chill" came over him, which seemed almost to freeze the very blood in his veins and gave him **intense agony**, from which he only found relief on awaking, having actually fallen asleep in that condition. Finally, however, he arrived at Philadelphia, on a steamer, Sabbath morning. A devoted friend of his, expecting him, **engaged** a carriage and **repaired** to the wharf for the box. The **bill of lading** and the receipt he had with him, and likewise knew where the box was located on the boat. Although he well knew freight was not usually delivered on Sunday, yet his deep **solicitude** for the safety of his friend determined him to do all that lay in his power to rescue him from his **perilous** situation. Handing his bill of lading to the proper officer of the boat, he asked if he could get the freight that it called for. The officer looked at the bill and said, "No, we do not deliver freight on Sunday;" but, noticing the anxiety of the man, he asked him if he would know it if he were to see it. Slowly— fearing that too much interest **manifested** might excite suspicion—he replied: "I think I should." Deliberately looking around amongst all the "freight," he discovered the box, and said, "I think that is it there." Said officer stepped to it, looked at the directions on it, then at the bill of lading, and said, "That is right, take it along." . . . But the size of the box was too large for the carriage, and the driver refused to take it. Nearly an hour and a half

season: time; period

revived: returned to consciousness

ordeal: difficult experience

intense: very strong

agony: suffering

engaged: hired

repaired: went

bill of lading: list of items shipped

solicitude: concern

perilous: dangerous

manifested: shown; displayed

William Jones was not the only slave who was mailed, undiscovered, out of the South. In 1848 Henry Brown was shipped in a three-foot trunk from Richmond, Virginia, to Philadelphia.

| 1850 Congress passes the Fugitive Slave Law requiring the return of runaway slaves. | 1860 An estimated 50,000 slaves have escaped since 1830 on the Underground Railroad. | 1861 The Civil War begins. |

In this broadside, or poster, a slave trader promises to pay top dollar for young men and women.

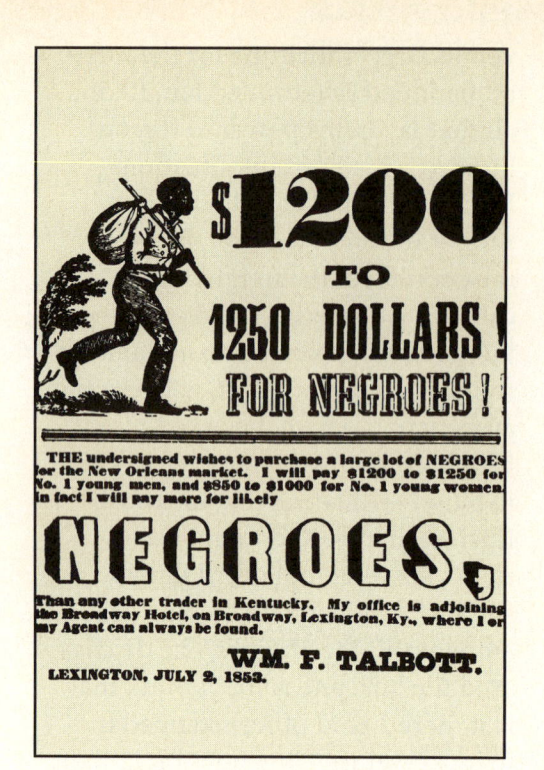

procured: obtained

agency: force; power

commenced: began

subsided: decreased

Rubicon: a point after which a decision cannot be changed

loosed: released

mortal: a person

abate: lessen

Vigilance Committee: Philadelphia group that helped slaves escape

partook: took part

trial: difficult situation; test

resolution: firm determination

Albany: capital city of New York

subjoined: added at the end

was spent in looking for a furniture car. Finally one was **procured**, and again the box was laid hold of by the occupant's particular friend, when, to his dread alarm, the poor fellow within gave a sudden cough. At this startling circumstance he dropped the box; equally as quick, although dreadfully frightened, and, as if helped by some invisible **agency**, he **commenced** singing, "Hush, my babe, lie still and slumber," with the most apparent indifference, at the same time slowly making his way from the box. Soon his fears **subsided**, and it was presumed that no one was any the wiser on account of the accident, or coughing. Thus, after summoning courage, he laid hold of the box a third time, and the **Rubicon** was passed. The car driver, totally ignorant of the contents of the box, drove to the number to which he was directed to take it—left it and went about his business. Now is a moment of intense interest—now of inexpressible delight. The box is opened, the straw removed, and the poor fellow is **loosed**; and is rejoicing, I will venture to say, as **mortal** never did rejoice, who had not been in similar peril. This particular friend was scarcely less overjoyed, however, and their joy did not **abate** for several hours; nor was it confined to themselves, for two invited members of the **Vigilance Committee** also **partook** of a full share. This box man was named Wm. Jones. He was boxed up in Baltimore by the friend who received him at the wharf, who did not come in the boat with him, but came in the cars and met him at the wharf.

The **trial** in the box lasted just seventeen hours before victory was achieved. Jones was well cared for by the Vigilance Committee and sent on his way rejoicing, feeling that **Resolution,** Underground Rail Road, and Liberty were invaluable.

On his way to Canada, he stopped at **Albany**, and the **subjoined** letter gives his view of things from that stand-point—

Slave dealers grew wealthy by transporting blacks from the North to the South and selling them for a profit.

Mr. Still:—I take this opportunity of writing a few lines to you hoping that **tha** may find you in good health and **femaly**. i am well at present and doing well at present i am now in a store and getting sixteen dollars a month at the present. i feel very much o blige to you and your family for your kindness to me while i was with you i have got a long without any **trub le a tal**. i am now in albany City. give my lov to mrs and mr miller and tel them i am very much a blige to them for there kind ns. give my lov to my Brother nore Jones tel him i should like to **here** from him very much and he must write. tel him to give my love to all of my perticular friends and tel them i should like to see them very much. tel him that he must come to see me for i want to see him for **sum thing** very **perticler**. please **ansure** this letter as soon as **posabul** and excuse me for not writing sooner as i dont write myself. no more at the present.

William Jones.

tha: (they)

femaly: (family)

trub le a tal: (trouble at all)

here: (hear)

sum thing: (something)

perticler: (particular)

ansure: (answer)

posabul: (possible)

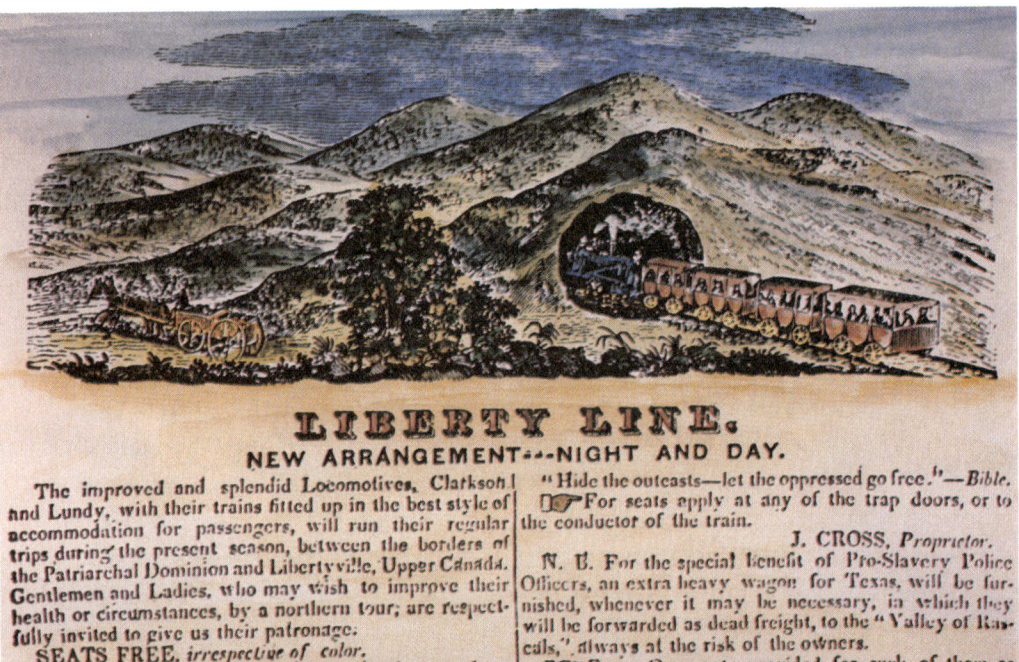

This advertisement for the Underground Railroad appeared in 1844 in a publication called the *Western Citizen*. It was a message to slaves looking for a way to escape.

After his stop in New York Peel continued on to Canada, using the alias William Jones. He remained a free man. William Still continued working for the Underground Railroad. After the Civil War Still wrote a book about the courage, the hardships, and the hopes that were a part of the antislavery movement in the United States.

From William Still, *Underground Rail Road*, pp. 28–30. Reprinted by permission of Johnson Publishing Company, Inc. Copyright © 1970 Ebony Classics.

UNIT 5

THE CIVIL WAR

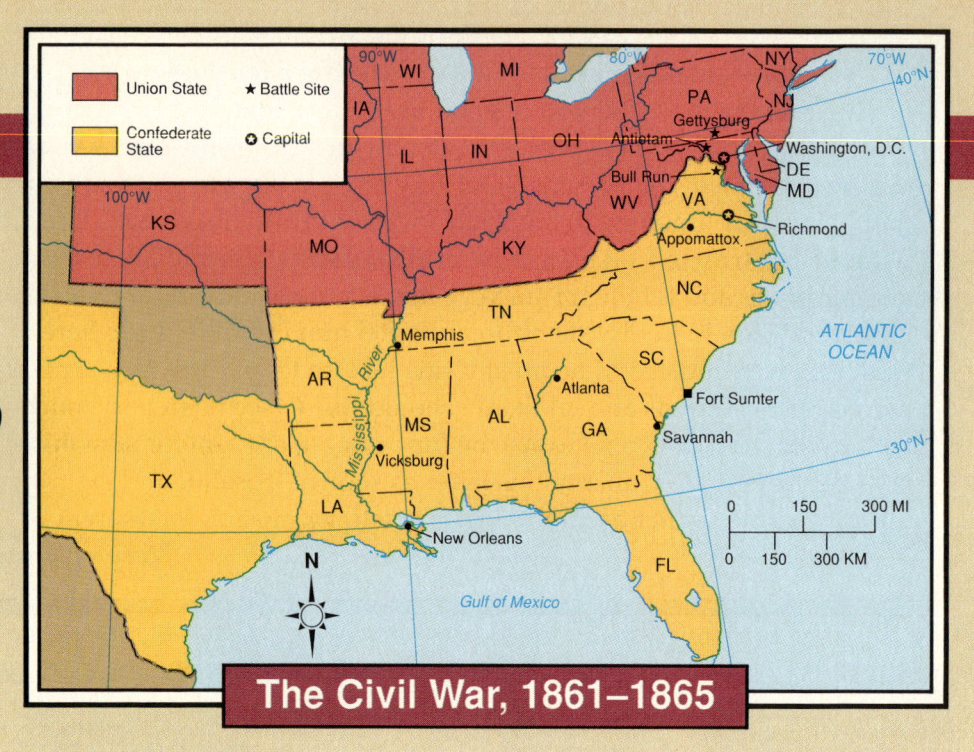

The Civil War, 1861–1865

Richmond: capital of the Confederacy, in Virginia

The opening shots of the Civil War were fired at Fort Sumter, South Carolina, in April 1861. Hoping for a short war President Lincoln called for 75,000 volunteers, and Confederate President Davis called for 100,000 men. When the war ended four years later, 2,900,000 men had served in the Union and Confederate armies. Almost one fourth lost their lives, and hundreds of thousands were wounded or permanently disabled.

Union troops won early victories in the West. There, under the leadership of General Ulysses S. Grant, Union forces captured several important forts. They also captured the cities of New Orleans and Memphis and gained control of much of the Mississippi River, a major supply line for the Confederacy.

In the East, Confederate troops under General Robert E. Lee had successfully defended **Richmond** from several Union attacks and won both Battles of Bull Run. Not until 1862, when Lee was forced to retreat at Antietam in Maryland, did Union troops win a major victory.

The costliest and bloodiest battle for both sides occurred July 1–3, 1863, near Gettysburg, Pennsylvania. This battle, along with the fall of Vicksburg on the Mississippi River in the same month, marked the

1861	1862	1863

1863 John Haley fights for the Union in the Battle of Gettysburg. Union forces win.

turning point of the war. Following these losses, the Confederacy had little hope of winning the war.

Impressed by Grant's success at Vicksburg, Lincoln appointed him general-in-chief of all the Union armies in 1864. Grant immediately began trying to wear down Lee's troops by repeated attacks. In Georgia General William Sherman began his march of destruction from Atlanta to Savannah. Under such military pressure the South could not last long.

Lee surrendered to Grant at Appomattox Court House, Virginia, on April 9, 1865. Other Confederate leaders gave up soon afterwards. The Civil War was over.

About 180,000 blacks served in the Union Army during the Civil War. Twenty-three were awarded the Medal of Honor for their bravery in combat.

In this unit three participants describe the Civil War they witnessed.

■ In his journal Union soldier **John Haley** shares his experiences at the Battle of Gettysburg.
■ **Mrs. Alfred Proctor Aldrich** describes what happened when Sherman's army camped in her Southern town.
■ **Ulysses S. Grant** writes about his meeting with Robert E. Lee at Appomattox Court House.

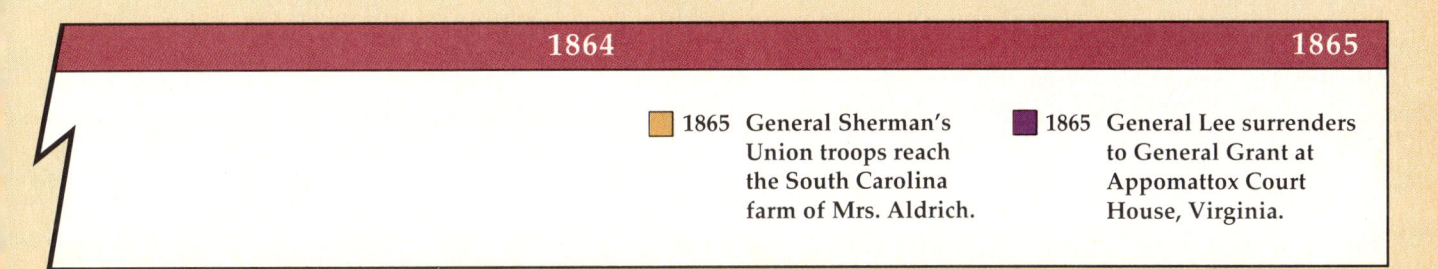

1864		1865
	■ 1865 General Sherman's Union troops reach the South Carolina farm of Mrs. Aldrich.	■ 1865 General Lee surrenders to General Grant at Appomattox Court House, Virginia.

51

Gettysburg Diary

"For two hours there was probably the greatest artillery duel ever fought on this planet."

John Haley

The South grew steadily weaker after its defeat at the Battle of Gettysburg in Pennsylvania.

In June 1863, after a string of victories in Virginia, Confederate General Robert E. Lee decided to take the war to the Northern states. The Southern army marched into Pennsylvania, hoping that a victory on Northern soil would force the Union to ask for peace. The armies collided at a small town called Gettysburg. The battle there, lasting three days, was the bloodiest of the war. Union soldier John Haley tells of the last day of the battle in his diary.

artillery: large guns, such as cannons

infantry: foot soldiers

seethed: was filled

solid shot: round cast-iron shells

spherical case shot: another kind of shell

hillocks: small hills or mounds

commenced: began

July 3rd.
... Shortly after noon there were signs of activity in the Confederate lines. **Artillery** was being massed on Seminary Ridge and the same was true of **infantry**, although the woods concealed them. About 1 o'clock the Rebel cannon opened on us, and ours were soon replying. For two hours there was probably the greatest artillery duel ever fought on this planet. The air **seethed** with old iron. Death and destruction were everywhere. Men and horses mangled and bleeding; trees, rocks, and fences ripped and torn. Shells, **solid shot**, and **spherical case shot** screamed, hissed, and rattled in every direction. Men hugged the ground and sought safety behind **hillocks**, boulders, ledges, stone walls, bags of grain—anything that could give or suggest shelter from this storm of death. ...

General Hunt, chief of artillery, ordered our gunners to cease firing in order to cool the guns. No sooner was this done than the Rebels, supposing they had silenced us, began to come out of the woods and form in line of battle.

As soon as all was ready, the column **commenced** the march. Our

1861		
1861 The Civil War begins. Lincoln calls for volunteers.	1862 John Haley volunteers for the Union army.	1863 Union forces win at Gettysburg. Haley describes the battle in his diary.

52

guns opened on them with solid shot and shells as soon as they were within range. This had no effect except to huddle them closer. As they drew nearer, our guns increased the **havoc** in their ranks. . . . But on they pressed, bravely and firmly, closing up on the colors as gap after gap opened in their ranks.

A **32-pounder** on **Round Top** fired down the line **obliquely** and took out as many as twenty **files**. Even this didn't **arrest** their progress. . . .

At this time the Confederates had reached the Emmettsburg road and, having two fences to climb, all suggestion of **alignment** was lost. They were now little other than a mob, but they came on and on. They were determined to come in spite of **grape**, **cannister**, and bullets. Our division and many others hastened to the scene to take part in the closing act of this drama.

On they pushed, delivering a **withering** fire. But our fire was equally destructive, and they soon presented a bloody and desperate appearance. No troops could resist the awful attack to which they were exposed. It was a sheet of fire, backed by a wall of steel. They couldn't reach the wall and *live*. . . .

By 4 o'clock the **repulse** was complete, the victory won. Thousands who two hours before were in the **flush of manhood** now lay dead, dying, or prisoners. The Confederates **staked** all and lost. . . .

At Pickett's Charge Confederate soldiers had only enough time to plant their flag before they were overrun by the Union army.

havoc: great destruction

32-pounder: large cannon

Round Top: hill beyond Gettysburg

obliquely: at a slanting angle

files: lines of soldiers

arrest: stop

alignment: arrangement in a line

grape: cluster of small iron balls fired from a cannon

cannister: container of lead or iron shot that scatters when fired from a cannon

withering: destructive

repulse: driving back an attack

flush of manhood: beginning of their adult lives

staked: risked

The Confederate attack that John Haley witnessed became known as "Pickett's Charge," after its commanding officer General George E. Pickett. Of the 15,000 Confederates that set out across the open field that day, only about half returned to their own lines. John Haley survived the battle and the war. He wrote two books about his wartime experiences.

From *The Rebel Yell & the Yankee Hurrah*, ed. Ruth L. Silliker (Camden, ME: Down East Books, 1985), pp. 103, 106. Reprinted by permission of the publisher.

1865

1865 The Confederacy surrenders. The Civil War ends.

When Sherman Marched

"As I ... looked at these first 'blue coats' approaching, I will not deny that my heart sank...."

Mrs. Alfred Proctor Aldrich

Union General William T. Sherman is best known for his march of destruction through Georgia.

Union General William T. Sherman began his famous "march to the sea" in November 1864. Sherman's army of 60,000 men advanced from Atlanta to Savannah, Georgia. From Savannah the army went north through the Carolinas. As they marched, the troops destroyed everything in their path. Mrs. Aldrich describes what happened when Sherman's army marched through her farm near Barnwell, South Carolina.

anticipated: expected

death-knell: bells rung at a funeral

Salkehatchie: river in South Carolina

detachment: troops on special duty

depredations: robberies; destruction

piazza: large, open porch along one or more sides of a house

forsook: left

intent: determined

Early in the morning of the 5th of February we heard the **anticipated** sounds like a **death-knell**, the bombarding of the fortifications on the **Salkehatchie**, three miles below our town. The first **detachment** that entered the town was Kilpatrick's Cavalry, which must have been some time in advance of the infantry. He made headquarters at the largest and best house, in the center of the town, leaving his soldiers to range for miles around the country, committing the most ruthless **depredations**. . . .

As I stood upon the **piazza** and looked at these first "blue coats" approaching, I will not deny that my heart sank within me, and I felt like falling, for I remembered the horrible accounts we had for months been listening to of the brutal treatment of the army to the women of Georgia in their march from Atlanta to Savannah. The courage of which I had always felt myself possessed, I confess, **forsook** me then and I prayed God to protect me and my little ones from the invaders. The first of the soldiers who rushed into the house seemed only **intent** on searching for food, and when the safe was opened to them, ate like hungry wolves.

1861	
1861 The Civil War begins.	1863 Grant forces the surrender of Vicksburg.

54

So soon, however, as they were satisfied, their tramp through the house began. By this time they were pouring in at every door, and without asking to have bureaus and wardrobes opened, broke with their bayonets every lock, tearing out the contents, in hunting for gold, silver, and jewels, all of which had been sent off weeks before. Finding nothing to satisfy their **cupidity** so far, they began turning over mattresses, tearing open feather-beds, and scattering the contents in the wildest confusion. . . .

When one swarm departed, another "more hungry" for spoil would file in. And so we lived for days and nights, with guns and bayonets flashing in our faces, and the coarse language of this mass of ruffians sounding in our ears.

One day a wretch who looked as if he had been brought from **Sing Sing** for the purpose of terrifying women and children, came into my piazza where I was standing surrounded by a more decent crowd than usual, carrying a rope in his hand, with which I learned afterwards he had three times hung up one of our servants, who had been reported to him as having aided me in hiding my silver. . . . With this rope shaken in my face, the monster said:

"Madame, if you do not tell me in five minutes where your silver is buried I will set fire to your home!"

Fortunately I had asked, not long before, a very gentlemanly looking soldier—there were *some* of this class, if Gen. Sherman permitted houses occupied by women and children to be burned? and I had been

cupidity: greed

Sing Sing: a state prison in New York

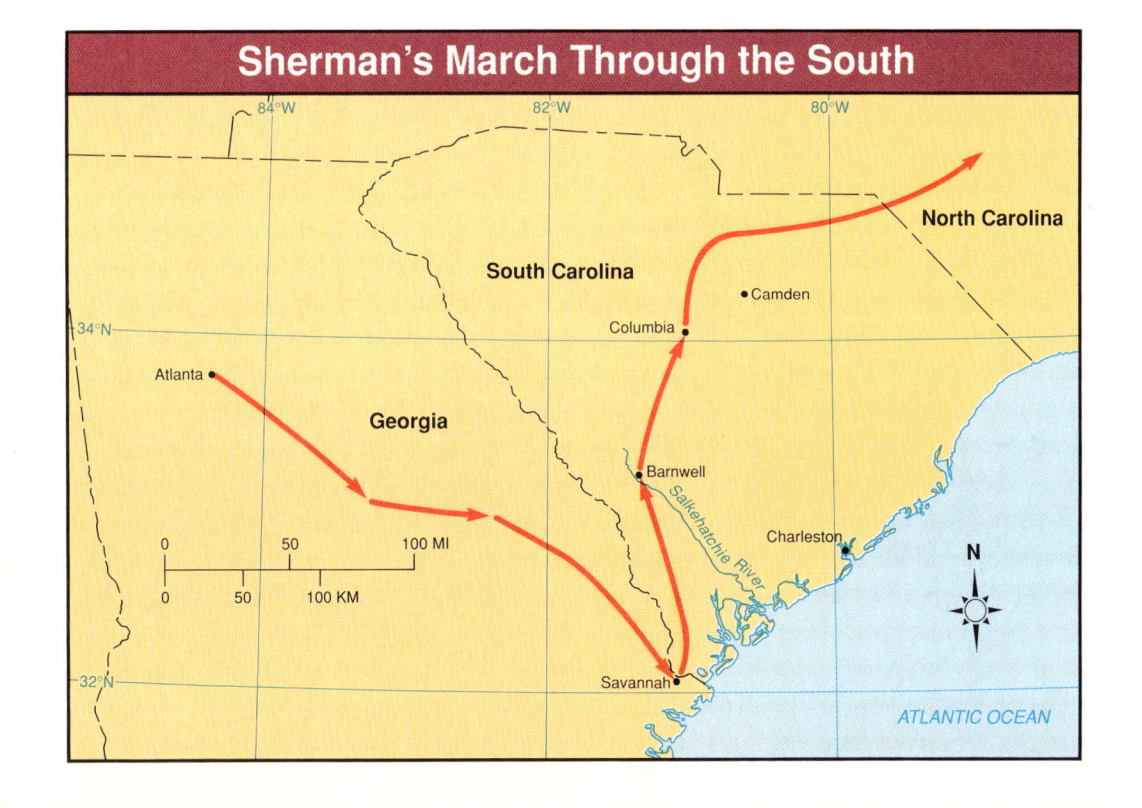

Sherman's March Through the South

| 1864 Sherman takes Atlanta and marches toward Savannah. | Feb. 1865 Sherman's troops march through South Carolina, looting the home of Mrs. Aldrich. | Apr. 1865 Sherman accepts the surrender of Confederate forces in North Carolina. |

Sherman's soldiers looted hundreds of homes in the South. They stole valuables, killed livestock, destroyed crops, and burned buildings to the ground.

Camden: city in South Carolina used as Confederate storehouse

disapprobation: feelings against; disapproval

fiend: evil spirit; demon

uncongenial: disagreeable

courtly: polite

told he did not. So I promptly replied to the ruffian.

"You dare not burn my house," I said, "for Gen. Sherman has forbidden it."

Just then I was greatly surprised to hear a voice at my back say: "Let the lady alone; you have no right to insult her after taking everything you could find. As to her silver, I can tell you it is not here; it has been sent to **Camden** for bank safety!"

I turned and looked at the pleasant, humane-looking face of this soldier in wonder and gratitude for his timely interference.

Soon my housekeeper came near and whispered: "I told him, and begged him to protect you from the wretch who was threatening you."

This good man stood nobly by us in several trying scenes after, and repeatedly expressed his **disapprobation** of war, and his sorrow for what he saw going on around him. Of his sincerity we could only hope. . . .

Almost the last division . . . was an Indiana regiment commanded by Gen. Hunter. . . . When I found the new arrivals pitching their tents by the front gate I sent at once to ask protection, and in reply was assured that I should be safe from intrusion. Very soon, however, the soldiers began to walk into the library, and help themselves to books and papers as they liked. After a while the General himself came in and drew a chair into the piazza, and with only a nod of his head to me, seated himself. His face I will never forget. It was that of a **fiend**. Several of his officers joined him. I have often thought they must have found him most **uncongenial**, for they were **courtly**, elegant gentlemen; two especially—Capt. Wheadon and the surgeon, whose name I have forgotten. They came to the library door and said most respectfully: "Good morning, madam."

A few moments after, one of the privates walked in and took an

56

armful of books from the book-case. I thought this did not look much like protection, and as he passed me going out, I stepped to the door and said:

"General, I understood you to say my house should be protected," pointing to the man with the second supply of books.

With a **sardonic** smile, he replied:

"The boys are all fond of reading. I guess they will not hurt the books."

Of course, I never saw them again. . . .

The next afternoon the news was brought me that the stables were on fire. Alongside of them was the corn house. I ran out to the General's tent, and found him seated outside, surrounded by his staff. They arose, with cap in hand, most respectfully. He kept his seat, his hat pulled over his eyes. . . . I **implored** him to come with me and have the fire extinguished. . . .

"For Heaven's sake, General, come and save my corn house. Surely you do not intend to destroy our last provisions and leave us to perish?"

At last he **reluctantly** arose and slowly followed me.

I hurried on, looking back and begging him to quicken his pace or it would be too late. When he got in speaking distance, he called out: "Boys, put out that fire."

A dozen or more "Boys" leaped the fence and soon extinguished it. . . .

He approached nearer to me and said:

"Madam, this is war—the war which you women helped to bring on yourselves."

"Yes," I said, "but we did not expect to deal with barbarians—rather with men who claimed to be **chivalrous** and honorable, and who have wives and children of their own.". . .

He laughed a laugh that rang in my ears long after, and said: "Madam, the end will soon come when we have finished our work in this State."

As he **struck** his tents and moved off, the corn-house I had tried so hard to save was discovered in flames. I always believed Gen. Hunter gave the order.

This photograph taken during the Civil War shows General Sherman (right foreground) meeting with his military staff in Atlanta.

sardonic: sarcastic

implored: begged

reluctantly: unwillingly

chivalrous: courteous, brave, and honest

struck: took down; took apart

The destruction caused by Sherman's army was especially savage in South Carolina. Soldiers destroyed war supplies, public buildings, railroads, and manufacturing shops. The troops took whatever supplies they needed from the nearby farms. Sherman wanted to destroy the South's **morale** as well as its resources. After the war Sherman succeeded Ulysses S. Grant as head of the United States Army.

morale: spirit; enthusiasm

Reprinted with permission of Macmillan Publishing Company from *When Sherman Came,* by Katharine M. Jones, pp. 114-16, 119-21. Copyright © 1964 Katharine M. Jones.

Surrender at Appomattox

“ Our conversation grew so pleasant that I almost forgot the object of our meeting. ”
Ulysses S. Grant

Confederate General Robert E. Lee (seated left) surrenders to General Ulysses S. Grant at Appomattox Court House in Virginia.

Mexican War: fought in 1846–1848 between the United States and Mexico

brigadier general: officer who ranks just above a colonel

memoirs: story of his life and experiences; autobiography

garb: clothing

blouse: loose-fitting shirt

Ulysses S. Grant graduated from West Point and served in the **Mexican War,** as did Robert E. Lee. When the Civil War began, Grant responded to Lincoln's call for volunteers and was appointed **brigadier general.** He won victories in the West and eventually was appointed to command all Union troops. In his **memoirs** Grant describes Lee's surrender in April 1865.

I had known General Lee in the old army, and had served with him in the Mexican War; but did not suppose, owing to the difference in our age and rank, that he would remember me; while I would more naturally remember him distinctly, because he was the chief of staff of General Scott in the Mexican War.

When I had left camp that morning I had not expected so soon the result that was then taking place, and consequently was in rough **garb.** I was without a sword, as I usually was when on horseback on the field, and wore a soldier's **blouse** for a coat, with the shoulder straps of my rank to indicate to the army who I was. When I went into the house I found General Lee. We greeted each other, and after shaking hands took our seats. I had my staff with me, a good portion of whom were in the room during the whole of the interview. . . .

General Lee was dressed in a full uniform which was entirely new, and was wearing a sword of considerable value, very likely the sword which had been presented by the State of Virginia; at all events, it was an entirely different sword from the

1861		
1861 The Civil War begins.	1862 Grant captures Confederate forts in Tennessee.	1863 Grant's victory at Vicksburg wins him Lincoln's confidence.

one that would ordinarily be worn in the field. In my rough traveling suit, the uniform of a private with the straps of a lieutenant-general, I must have contrasted very strangely with a man so handsomely dressed, six feet high and of faultless form. But this was not a matter that I thought of until afterwards.

We soon fell into a conversation about old army times. He remarked that he remembered me . . . and I told him that as a matter of course I remembered him perfectly. . . . Our conversation grew so pleasant that I almost forgot the object of our meeting. After the conversation had run on in this style for some time, General Lee called my attention to the object of our meeting, and said that he had asked for this interview for the purpose of getting from me the terms I proposed to give his army. I said that I meant merely that his army should **lay down their arms**, not to take them up again during the **continuance** of the war unless **duly and properly exchanged**. . . .

I . . . **commenced** writing out the following terms:

lay down their arms: put down their weapons; stop fighting

continuance: remainder

duly and properly exchanged: done according to standard procedure or custom

commenced: began

Appomattox C. H., VA.,
Ap'l 9th, 1865.

Gen. R. E. Lee,
Comd'g C. S. A.

Gen: In accordance with the substance of my letter to you of the 8th inst., I propose to receive the surrender of the Army of N. Va. on the following terms, **to wit**: Rolls of all the officers and men to be made in duplicate. . . . The officers to give their individual **paroles** not to take up arms against the Government of the United States until properly exchanged, and each company or regimental commander sign a like parole for the men of their commands. The arms, **artillery** and public property to be parked and stacked, and turned over to the officer appointed by me to receive them. This will not **embrace** the **side-arms** of the officers, nor their private horses or baggage. This done, each officer and man will be allowed to return to their homes, not to be disturbed by United States authority so long as they observe their paroles and the laws in force where they may reside.

Very respectfully,
U. S. Grant,
Lt. Gen.

Comd'g C.S.A.: Commanding Confederate States of America

to wit: that is to say

paroles: words of honor

artillery: large guns, such as cannons

embrace: include

side-arms: swords, revolvers, or other weapons worn at the side or in the belt

---

1864 Lincoln appoints Grant commander of all Union forces. Grant's army repeatedly attacks Lee's forces in Virginia.

1865 Grant accepts the surrender of Lee at Appomattox, Virginia.

effects: belongings

kindred subjects: similar topics

When I put my pen to the paper I did not know the first word that I should make use of in writing the terms. I only know what was in my mind, and I wished to express it clearly, so that there could be no mistaking it. As I wrote on, the thought occurred to me that the officers had their own private horses and **effects**, which were important to them, but of no value to us; also that it would be an unnecessary humiliation to call upon them to deliver their side arms.

No conversation, not one word, passed between General Lee and myself, either about private property, side arms, or **kindred subjects**. He appeared to have no objections to the terms first proposed. . . . When he read over that part of the terms about side arms, horses and private property of the officers, he remarked, with some feeling, I thought, that this would have a happy effect upon his army. . . .

He then sat down and wrote out the following letter:

stipulations: conditions of the agreement

> *Headquarters Army of Northern Virginia,*
> *April 9, 1865.*
>
> General:—I received your letter of this date containing the terms of the surrender of the Army of Northern Virginia as proposed by you. As they are substantially the same as those expressed in your letter of the 8th inst., they are accepted. I will proceed to designate the proper officers to carry the **stipulations** into effect.
>
> R. E. Lee, General.

After the surrender General Lee bid farewell to his troops. Many soldiers returned home to find that their property had been damaged during the war.

While duplicates of the two letters were being made, the Union generals present were **severally** presented to General Lee.

The much talked of surrendering of Lee's sword and my handing it back, this and much more that has been said about it is the purest **romance**. The word sword or side arms was not mentioned by either of us until I wrote it in the terms. . . .

General Lee, after all was completed and before taking his leave, remarked that his army was in a very bad condition for want of food, and that they were without **forage**; that his men had been living for some days on parched corn exclusively, and that he would have to ask me for rations and forage. I told him "certainly," and asked for how many men he wanted rations. His answer was "about twenty-five thousand:" and I authorized him to send his own **commissary** and **quartermaster** to Appomattox Station . . . where he could have, out of the trains we had stopped, all the provisions wanted. . . .

Lee and I then separated as cordially as we had met. . . .

Soon after Lee's departure I telegraphed to Washington as follows:

severally: individually; separately

romance: fiction

forage: grain or other food for horses

commissary: officer in charge of military supplies

quartermaster: officer who deals with food and supplies for troops

---

Headquarters Appomattox C. H., VA.,
April 9th, 1865, 4:30 P.M.

Hon. E. M. Stanton, Secretary of War, Washington.

General Lee surrendered the Army of Northern Virginia this afternoon on terms proposed by myself. The accompanying additional correspondence will show the conditions fully.

U. S. Grant,
Lieut.-General.

When news of the surrender first reached our lines our men commenced firing a salute of a hundred guns in honor of the victory. I at once sent word, however, to have it stopped. The Confederates were now our prisoners, and we did not want to **exult** over their downfall.

exult: rejoice

Three days after the meeting between Lee and Grant, the Confederate Army of Northern Virginia formally surrendered its weapons and battle flags to the Union forces. After the war Grant served two terms as president of the United States. In his later years Grant had financial problems. He wrote his memoirs, in part, to cover his losses from business failures.

From *Personal Memoirs of U. S. Grant*, with an introduction by Philip Van Doren Stern (Gloucester, MA: Peter Smith, 1969), pp. 425–29.

UNIT 6

THE CHANGING FRONTIER

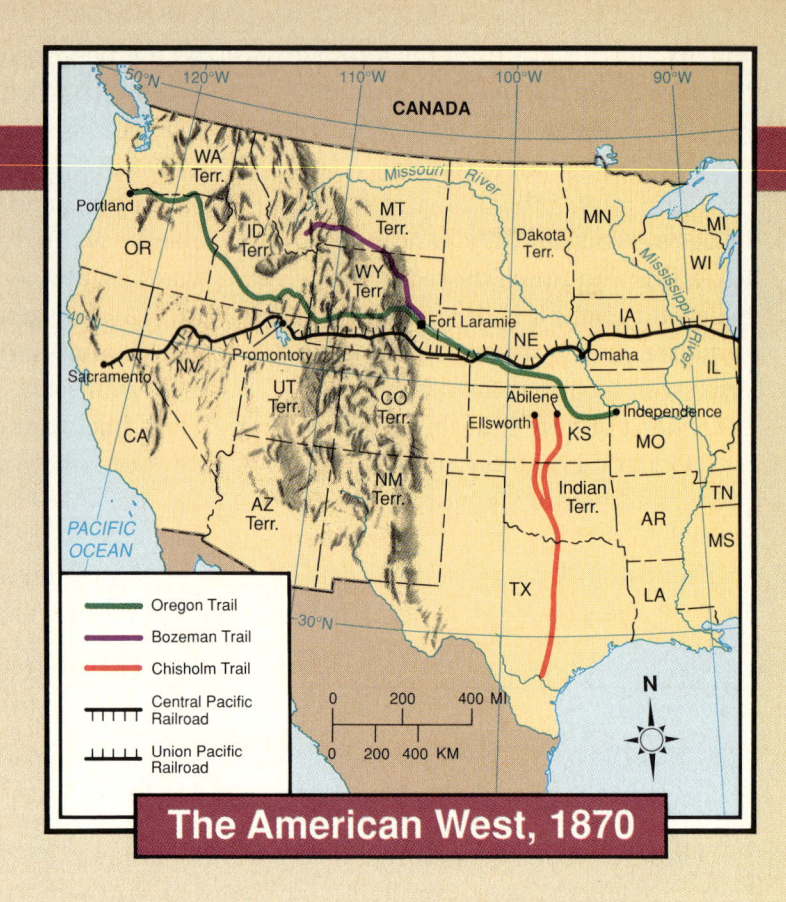

The American West, 1870

transcontinental: extending across a continent

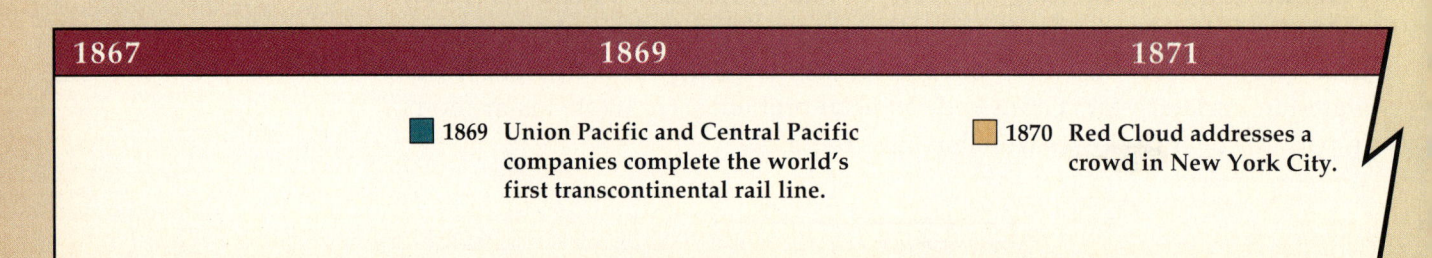

In the late 1800s a new era of growth and development began in the United States. The population tripled. Thousands of immigrants came to America from southern and eastern Europe. Some stayed in the cities in the East, and some pushed westward with the telegraph lines and railroads.

Railroads began to play a major role in shaping the movement of both the frontier and the population. By 1835 a thousand miles of railroad track serviced the cities along the east coast of the United States. In the 1860s two government-backed rail companies used more than six million ties to build the world's first **transcontinental** railroad. The railroad spike that connected the East and West lines was hammered into the rails at Promontory Point, Utah, in 1869.

For most people in the West the arrival of the railroad meant an increased flow of goods and improved passenger service. However, it had a devastating effect on Native Americans. The railroads helped to draw even more settlers to the West. The Native Americans watched the

1867	1869	1871
	■ 1869 Union Pacific and Central Pacific companies complete the world's first transcontinental rail line.	■ 1870 Red Cloud addresses a crowd in New York City.

stream of white pioneers that poured across their plains. To defend the land on which they had lived for centuries, the Native Americans fought against the white pioneers. They **sabotaged** the rails and the telegraph wires in an effort to stop the flow of intruders. But the Native Americans could not stop the thousands who followed the railroads west. By 1886 Native Americans—their numbers cut by two-thirds since the settlers first landed in America—were restricted to reservations.

The railroad expansion also affected the life of the cowboy. A cowboy's job was to drive Texas-bred cattle to the railroad stations in Kansas—a thousand miles away—and load them on eastbound trains. But as companies began to lay rails directly to the cattle ranches, the age of the cattle drive ended. Many American cowboys then turned to jobs as ranch hands.

sabotaged: destroyed

American artist Frederic Remington captured the spirit of the West in his paintings and sculptures. This painting is entitled *The Coming and Going of the Pony Express.*

In this unit three eyewitnesses describe the conditions in the American West at this time of growth and change.

- Journalist **Sidney Dillon** describes the scene of the last spike driven for the first transcontinental railroad.
- Oglala Sioux **Chief Red Cloud** speaks of justice in his speech at a New York rally.
- In his memoirs former cowboy **W. S. James** writes about the cowboy's style of clothing.

1873   **1875**   **1877**

■ 1875   Cattle ranches have spread across the Great Plains from Texas to Montana.

Driving the Golden Spike

" . . . the spike will soon be driven."
Sidney Dillon

Railroad officials and workers gathered to celebrate the completion of the first transcontinental railroad line in 1869.

point of junction: place where the Union Pacific and Central Pacific rail lines met

bustle: much moving around

Governor Stanford: governor of California, a Union Pacific director

President of the United States: Ulysses S. Grant

General Dodge: chief engineer of the Union Pacific

laurel: small evergreen tree

centre: middle

From Nebraska the Union Pacific rail line crews worked westward. From California the Central Pacific's crews worked eastward. They overcame floods, fires, and blizzards to make this railroad. When completed it would be the first to join the nation from coast to coast. On May 10, 1869, crews and officials met at Promontory Point, Utah, to drive in the last spike—a golden one. Journalist Sidney Dillon described the event.

The **point of junction** was in a level circular valley, about three miles in diameter, surrounded by mountains. During all the morning hours the hurry and **bustle** of preparation went on. Two lengths of rails lay on the ground near the opening in the road-bed. At a little before eleven the Chinese laborers began levelling up the road-bed preparatory to placing the last ties in position. About a quarter past eleven the train from San Francisco, bringing **Governor Stanford** and party arrived and was greeted with cheers. In the enthusiasm of the occasion there were cheers for everybody, from the **President of the United States** to the day-laborers on the road.

The two engines moved nearer each other, and the crowd gathered round the open space. . . . Brief remarks were made by Governor Stanford on one side, and **General Dodge** on the other. It was now about twelve o'clock noon, local time, or about 2 P.M. in New York. The two superintendents of construction . . . placed under the rails the last tie. It was of California **laurel**, highly polished, with a silver plate in the **centre** bearing the following inscription:

1862

| 1862 Pacific Railway Act charters two companies to lay tracks between the West Coast and the Midwest. | 1863 Central Pacific company lays tracks eastward from Sacramento. | 1865 Union Pacific company begins laying tracks westward from Omaha. |

"The last tie laid on the completion of the Pacific Railroad, May 10, 1869," with the names of the officers and directors of both companies.

Everything being then in readiness the word was given, and "Hats off" went clicking over the wires to the waiting crowds at New York, Philadelphia, San Francisco, and all the principal cities. Prayer was offered by the **venerable** Rev. Dr. Todd, at the conclusion of which our operator tapped out: "We have got done praying. The spike is about to be presented," to which the response came back: "We understand. All are ready in the East." The gentlemen who had been **commissioned** to present the four spikes, two of gold, and two of silver, from Montana, Idaho, California, and Nevada, stepped forward, and with brief appropriate remarks **discharged the duty** assigned them.

Governor Stanford, standing on the north, and Dr. Durant on the south side of the track, received the spikes and put them in place. Our operator tapped out: "All ready now; the spike will soon be driven. The signal will be three dots for the **commencement** of the blows." An instant later the silver hammers came down, and at each stroke in all the offices from San Francisco to New York, and throughout the land, the hammer of the magnet struck the bell. . . .

There was not much formality in the demonstration that followed, but the enthusiasm was genuine. . . . The two engines moved up until they touched each other, and a bottle of champagne was poured on the last rail, after the manner of christening a ship at the launching. . . .

venerable: term of respect meaning worthy of reverence

commissioned: given the duty

discharged the duty: performed the task

commencement: beginning

As railroads spread across the West, towns began to spring up along their trail.

The Union Pacific and Central Pacific transcontinental rail line connected the many Eastern lines with the West. Other cross-country railroad lines were soon built. Government loans and generous land grants made construction possible. The railroad companies sold part of the land to settlers. The companies also built towns and encouraged others to build towns along the routes. The railroads were a major factor in the settlement of the American West.

From Sidney Dillon, "Historic Moment: Driving the Last Spike," *Scribner's Magazine*, XII (August, 1892), pp. 258–59.

| 1869 First transcontinental rail line is formed by connecting Central and Union Pacifics in Utah. | 1883 Four transcontinental rail lines have been completed across the United States. | 1890 Over 70,000 miles of track have been laid between the Mississippi River and the Pacific Ocean. |

Justice for All

" I am a representative of the original American race.... "

Chief Red Cloud

Chief Red Cloud tried to keep the lands of the Oglala Sioux from becoming a highway to the West for European settlers.

In the late 1800s Plains tribes fought to keep their lands and their way of life. They found, however, that the tide of settlers and soldiers flooding onto their lands could not be held back. In 1870 Red Cloud, a chief of the Oglala Sioux, spoke at a rally in New York City. He expressed his desire for acceptance, mutual respect, and justice for Native Americans.

brethren: brothers and sisters

disposed to: aware of

My **brethren** and my friends who are here before me this day, God Almighty has made us all, and He is here to bless what I have to say to you today. The Good Spirit made us both. He gave you lands and He gave us lands; He gave us these lands; you came in here, and we respected you as brothers. God Almighty made you but made you all white and clothed you; when He made us He made us with red skins and poor; now you have come.

When you first came we were very many, and you were few; now you are many, and we are getting very few, and we are poor. You do not know who appears before you today to speak. I am a representative of the original American race, the first people of this continent. We are good and not bad. The reports that you hear concerning us are all on one side. We are always **disposed to** them. You are here told that we are traders and thieves, and it is not so. We have given you nearly all our lands, and if we had any more land to give we would be very glad to give it. We have nothing more. We are driven into a very little land, and we want you now, as our dear friends, to help us with the government of the United States....

1852

1852 Plains tribes sign treaty allowing travelers to pass through their territories.

1863 Thousands of white settlers use Bozeman Trail through Sioux hunting grounds.

You have children; we have children. You want to raise your children and make them happy and prosperous; we want to raise [ours] and make them happy and prosperous. We ask you to help us to do it.

At the mouth of the **Horse Creek**, in 1852, the **Great Father** made a treaty with us by which we agreed to let all that country open for fifty-five years for the **transit** of those who were going through. We kept this treaty; we never treated any man wrong; we never committed any murder or **depredation** until afterward the troops were sent into that country, and the troops killed our people and ill-treated them, and thus war and trouble arose; but before the troops . . . we were quiet and peaceable. . . .

In 1868 men came out and brought papers. We are ignorant and do not read papers, and they did not tell us right what was in these papers. . . . The interpreters deceived us. When I went to Washington I saw the Great Father. The Great Father showed me what the treaties were; he showed me all these points and showed me that the interpreters had deceived me and did not let me know what the right side of the treaty was. All I want is right and justice. . . . I represent the Sioux Nation; they will be governed by what I say and what I represent. . . .

I am going back home. I am very glad that you have listened to me, and I wish you good-bye and give you an affectionate farewell.

Horse Creek: tributary of North Platte River on Native American land south of Fort Laramie

Great Father: Millard Fillmore, who was president of the United States at the time

transit: passage

depredation: great destruction

Chief Red Cloud (far left) joined other Sioux and Arapaho leaders on trips to Washington, D.C., to represent the interests of their people.

Red Cloud, the only Western chief to win a long war against United States troops, made several trips to the East after 1868. He spoke to audiences for peace while other chiefs called for war. Red Cloud knew the Sioux were outnumbered. He told an official, "Our nation is melting away like the snow on the sides of the hills where the sun is warm, while your people are like the blades of grass in the spring when the summer is coming."

From *Great Documents in American Indian History*, Wayne Moquin, ed., with Charles Van Doren (Praeger Publishers, New York, 1973), pp. 211–13. Copyright © 1973 by Praeger Publishers, Inc. Reprinted with permission.

1866 Red Cloud walks out on peace treaty talks. The Oglala Sioux go to war.

1868 Red Cloud signs a peace treaty with the United States. He and his people move to reservation lands.

1870 Red Cloud speaks at a rally in New York City.

Cowboy Style

" The cowboy's outfit . . . is of the very best from hat to boots. . . . "

W. S. James

The cowboy's "uniform" included a broad-brimmed hat, vest, chaps, bandanna, and heavy leather boots. His six-shooters came in handy for killing rattlesnakes or controlling cattle stampedes.

To most people a cowboy is a hard-riding, fast-shooting American hero of the 1870s. But in fact tending cattle meant long hours at hard, dirty jobs to earn about $30 a month. The cowboy's outfit was selected for its usefulness. Cowboys chose clothes for protection against rattlesnakes, thorny brush, and the weather. W. S. James describes cowboy style in his memoirs of cowboy life.

war: Civil War

enterprising: ambitious; creative

leggins: coverings for the trousers; chaps

substantial: better than average

The cow-boy goes to the school of nature, learns his lesson from observation and practical experience. . . .

During the **war** his clothing was made from home-spun cloth, he had no other, home-made shoes or boots, even his hat was homemade, the favorite hat material being straw. . . . Sometimes a fellow would get hold of a Mexican hat, and then he was sailing.

The popular way for protecting the clothing, was to make a leather cap for the knee and seat of the pants, the more **enterprising** would make **leggins** of calf-skin, hair out, and sometimes buckskin with fringe down the side. . . .

If you see him in New York or Chicago you see him wearing the same sort of a hat and boots he wears at home. . . .

The cow-boy's outfit of clothing, as a rule, is of the very best from hat to boots, he may not have a dollar in the world, but he will wear good, **substantial** clothing, even if he has to buy it on a credit, and he usually has plenty of that, that is good. . . .

1867		
1867 Chisholm Trail opens as a cattle trail from southern Texas to Kansas railroad towns.	**1871** Cowboys trail drive 600,000 cattle north to markets.	**1874** Settlers begin using barbed wire fencing against open-range cattle.

After a long day cowboys gathered at the chuck wagon for their evening meal. The cook was a cowboy's best friend, serving up food and often playing the role of barber, seamstress, and nurse.

Cowboy Nat Love gained fame for his riding, roping, and shooting ability.

A cowboy's rope, or lariat, was one of his most important tools. A skillfully thrown lasso could bring down a steer for branding or snag a runaway horse.

By 1890 the wide-open cattle country was being divided and fenced for farmland and ranches. The expansion of railroads limited the need for long cattle drives and cowboys. Though the work had become less demanding, the cowboy's need for practical, durable clothing continued. The rugged American cowboy image and clothing style of boots, jeans, and hats remain fashionable today.

From *Cowboy Life: Reconstructing an American Myth*, pp. 113, 118–19. Edited and with an introduction by William W. Savage, Jr. Copyright © 1975 by the University of Oklahoma Press.

| 1880 | In this decade open-range cattle-raising ends, and the Great Plains becomes a farming region. | 1883 | "Buffalo Bill" Cody opens his touring Wild West Show to display cowboy skills. |

69

UNIT 7

REFORMS IN A NEW CENTURY

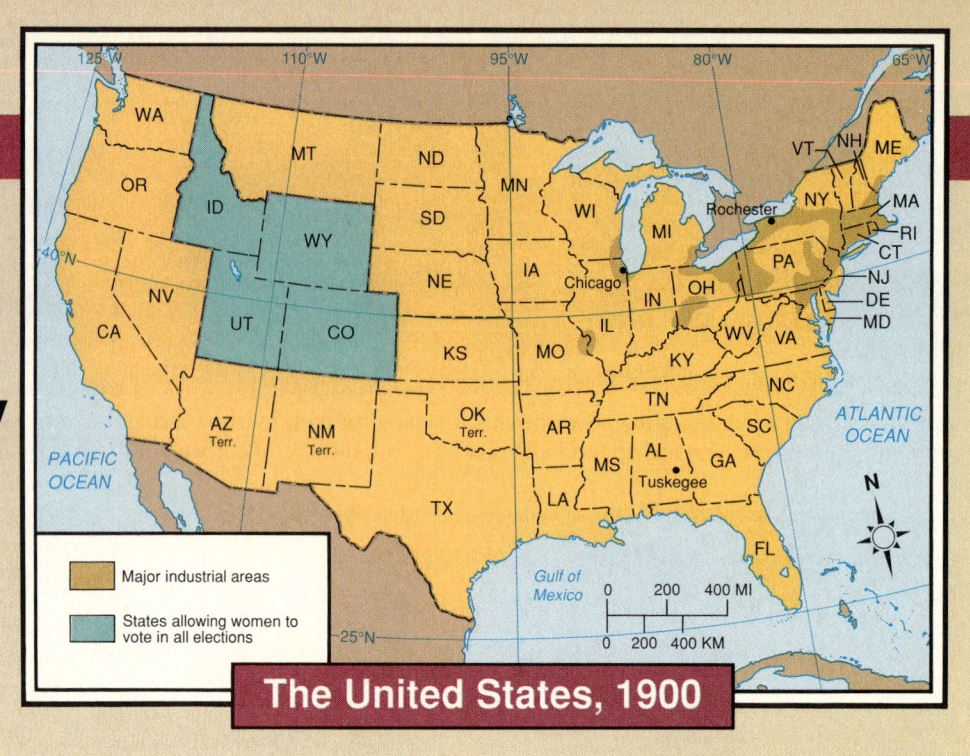

The United States, 1900

- Major industrial areas
- States allowing women to vote in all elections

The beginning of the new century was cheered by many people in the United States. Some had much to celebrate. Business was booming. Railroads crisscrossed the country. The population of some American cities, such as New York, Philadelphia, and Chicago, had grown to over one million people each. But not all Americans shared equally in the wealth of the nation. The late nineteenth century in America has been called the "Gilded Age." Like a piece of ornamentation that is gold on the outside but cheap underneath, American society appeared prosperous and satisfied, but a closer look revealed corruption and injustice.

Many black Americans faced conditions that cried out for reform. The Fifteenth Amendment, passed in 1870, guaranteed black men the right to vote. However, several Southern states tried to prevent blacks from exercising their newly won rights. Southern blacks often found themselves blocked from polling places. Many continued to struggle without land, money, or education.

Women did not share all of America's freedoms. At the turn of the century only four states granted women suffrage, or allowed them to vote. It was not until the Nineteenth Amendment was passed in 1920 that all women were guaranteed the right to vote. This change took

| 1870 | 1880 | 1890 |

■ 1872 Susan B. Anthony is arrested in Rochester, New York, for voting in the presidential election.

place only after women's organizations had dedicated years to protest and activism.

The industrialized cities of the Northern states developed problems and injustices, too. For many years factories employed children because they provided cheap labor. Adults and children alike faced dangerous and unregulated conditions in sweatshops and factories. Their plight was championed by a group of reformers known as the Progressives. The Progressives helped to end child labor, improve working conditions in America's factories, and reform corrupt local governments. They wrote books and published magazine articles. They also campaigned for laws to enforce reforms.

The growth of industry in the late 1800s led to abuses in the work place. In 1860 female shoemakers walked off the job in Massachusetts to protest working conditions.

In this unit three people tell about the challenges they faced during the years of reform in America.

- In the court transcription from her trial, **Susan B. Anthony** defends her attempt to vote.
- **George Washington Carver** relates his early years and his love of learning in an autobiographical account.
- In a passage from *The Jungle,* **Upton Sinclair** describes the sickening conditions in the meat-packing industry.

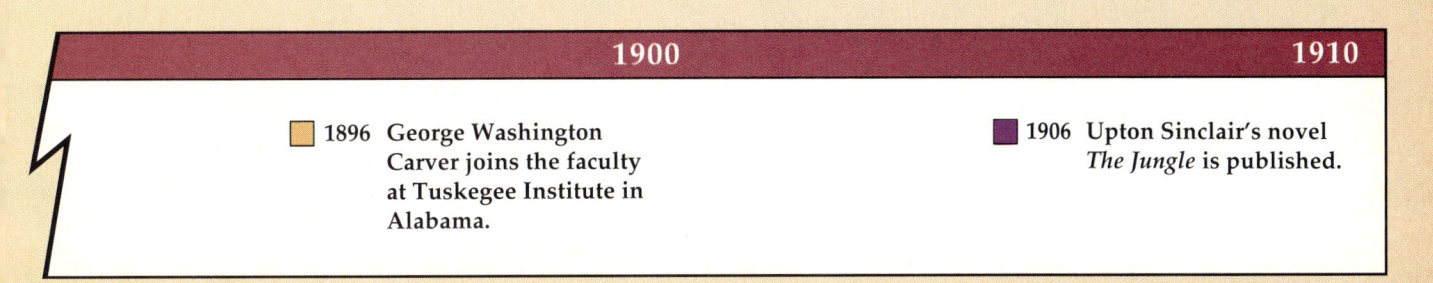

1900 **1910**

- 1896 George Washington Carver joins the faculty at Tuskegee Institute in Alabama.
- 1906 Upton Sinclair's novel *The Jungle* is published.

Guilty of Voting

" My natural rights, my civil rights, my political rights, my judicial rights, are all alike ignored."

Susan B. Anthony

Susan B. Anthony was an early crusader for women's rights.

American women were at one time forbidden by state laws to vote. On November 5, 1872, Susan B. Anthony broke the New York state law by casting a ballot in a Rochester, New York, election. She stood trial for her crime in Judge Ward Hunt's court. First the judge refused to let her testify. Then he ordered the jury to find her guilty. In this trial transcript Susan B. Anthony expresses her outrage.

ordered verdict: decision the judge ordered the jury to make in this trial

degraded: lowered

subject: person under the authority or control of another

subjection: control by others

counsel: lawyer

JUDGE HUNT—(Ordering the defendant to stand up) Has the prisoner anything to say why sentence shall not be pronounced?

MISS ANTHONY—Yes, your honor, I have many things to say; for in your **ordered verdict** of guilty, you have trampled under foot every vital principle of our government. My natural rights, my civil rights, my political rights, my judicial rights, are all alike ignored. Robbed of the fundamental privilege of citizenship, I am **degraded** from the status of a citizen to that of a **subject**; and not only myself individually, but all of my sex, are, by your honor's verdict, doomed to political **subjection** under this, so-called, form of government.

JUDGE HUNT—The Court cannot listen to . . . arguments the prisoner's **counsel** has already consumed three hours in presenting.

MISS ANTHONY—May it please your honor, I am not arguing the question, but simply stating the reasons why sentence cannot, in justice, be pronounced against me. Your denial of my citizen's right to vote, is the denial

1851		
1851 Susan B. Anthony meets Elizabeth Cady Stanton, a women's rights movement leader.	**1868** Anthony publishes a newspaper, *The Revolution*, which demands equal rights for women.	**1872** Anthony is arrested for voting in Rochester, New York.

of my right of consent as one of the governed, the denial of my right of representation as one of the taxed, the denial of my right to a trial by a jury of my **peers** as an offender against law, therefore, the denial of my sacred rights to life, liberty, property and—

JUDGE HUNT—The Court cannot allow the prisoner to go on.

MISS ANTHONY—But your honor will not deny me this one and only poor privilege of protest against this high-handed outrage upon my citizen's rights. May it please the Court to remember that since the day of my arrest last November, this is the first time that either myself or any person of my **disfranchised class** has been allowed a word of defense before judge or jury—

JUDGE HUNT—The prisoner must sit down—the Court cannot allow it.

MISS ANTHONY—All of my prosecutors, from the 8th **ward** corner grocery politician, who **entered the complaint**, to the United States Marshal, Commissioner, District Attorney, District Judge, your honor on the bench, not one is my peer, . . . and had your honor submitted my case to the jury, as was clearly your duty, even then I should have had just cause of protest, for not one of those men was my peer; but, native or foreign born, white or black, rich or poor, educated or ignorant, awake or asleep, sober or drunk, each and every man of them was my political superior; hence, in no sense, my peer. Even, under such circumstances, a **commoner** of England, tried before a jury of **Lords**, would have far less cause to complain than should I, a woman, tried before a jury of men. Even my counsel, **the Hon.** Henry R. Selden, who has argued my cause so ably, so earnestly, so unanswerably before your honor, is my political **sovereign**. Precisely as no disfranchised person is entitled to sit upon a jury, and no woman is entitled to the **franchise**, so, none but a regularly admitted lawyer is allowed to practice in the courts, and no

peers: equals

disfranchised class: group deprived of their right to vote

ward: voting unit

entered the complaint: made the formal complaint that caused the arrest

commoner: person who is not a member of the nobility

Lords: British title given to some men of high rank

the Hon.: (the Honorable) a title of respect

sovereign: superior

franchise: right to vote

By 1915 women could vote without restriction in 12 states. This poster urges the state of Massachusetts to follow suit.

1892 Anthony is elected president of the National American Woman Suffrage Association.

1920 Nineteenth Amendment guarantees women the right to vote.

Anthony (left) and Elizabeth Cady Stanton were long-time friends and partners in their struggle for equal rights.

gain admission to the bar: become a lawyer

it: freedom

mine: right to a voice

broad and liberal: general, loose, not literal

naturalized: made citizens

leniency: kindness

rigors: harsh judgment

woman can **gain admission to the bar**—hence, jury, judge, counsel, must all be of the superior class.

JUDGE HUNT—The Court must insist—the prisoner has been tried according to the established forms of law.

MISS ANTHONY—Yes, your honor, but by forms of law all made by men, interpreted by men, administered by men, in favor of men, and against women; and hence, your honor's ordered verdict of guilty, against a United States citizen for the exercise of *"that citizen's right to vote,"* simply because that citizen was a woman and not a man. But yesterday, the same man . . . declared it a crime punishable with $1,000 fine and six months' imprisonment, for . . . any of us, to give a cup of cold water, a crust of bread, or a night's shelter to a panting fugitive as he was tracking his way to Canada. And every man or woman in whose veins coursed a drop of human sympathy violated that wicked law . . . and was justified in so doing. As then, the slaves who got their freedom must take **it** over, or under, or through the unjust forms of law, precisely so, now, must women, to get their right to a voice in this government, take it; and I have taken **mine**, and mean to take it at every possible opportunity.

JUDGE HUNT—The Court orders the prisoner to sit down. It will not allow another word.

MISS ANTHONY—When I was brought before your honor for trial, I hoped for a **broad and liberal** interpretation of the Constitution . . . that should declare equality of rights the national guarantee to all persons born or **naturalized** in the United States. But failing to get this justice—failing, even, to get a trial by a jury *not* of my peers—I ask not **leniency** at your hands—but rather the full **rigors** of the law.

JUDGE HUNT—The Court must insist—

(Here the prisoner sat down.)

JUDGE HUNT—The prisoner will stand up.

(Here Miss Anthony arose again.)

The sentence of the Court is that you pay a fine of one hundred dollars and the costs of the prosecution.

MISS ANTHONY—May it please your honor, I shall never pay a dollar of your unjust penalty. All the stock in trade I possess is a $10,000 debt,

Women continued to fight for equal rights long after Anthony's death in 1906. This suffragist parade was held in New York City in 1912.

incurred by publishing my paper—*The Revolution*—four years ago, the sole object of which was to educate all women to do precisely as I have done, rebel against your man-made, unjust, unconstitutional forms of law, that tax, fine, imprison and hang women, while they deny them the right of representation in the government; and I shall work on with might and main to pay every dollar of that honest debt, but not a penny shall go to this unjust claim. And I shall earnestly and persistently continue to urge all women to the practical recognition of the old revolutionary **maxim**, that "Resistance to **tyranny** is obedience to God."

JUDGE HUNT—Madam, the Court will not order you **committed** until the fine is paid.

incurred: brought about

The Revolution: a women's rights newspaper

maxim: saying

tyranny: harsh and unjust rule

committed: jailed

Judge Hunt purposely refused to send Susan B. Anthony to jail. Without a jail sentence Anthony could not ask a higher court to review the decision. Therefore, she had to live with her conviction. She never did pay the fine. Anthony continued the fight for women's rights. Fourteen years after her death the Nineteenth Amendment was passed, giving women the right to vote.

From *An Account of the Proceedings on the Trial of Susan B. Anthony* (New York: Arno Press, 1974), pp. 81–85.

A Brief Sketch of My Life

"When just a mere tot . . . my very soul thirsted for an education."

George Washington Carver

George Washington Carver believed that if the economy of the South improved, the status of blacks would also improve.

George Washington Carver was born just before the close of the Civil War. Many hardships still existed for his family and other newly freed slaves. But opportunities were becoming available for freed slaves to pursue a better life. As a very young child Carver displayed a great interest in plants and a desire to learn. In this brief autobiographical sketch he describes his life and education before he became a famous scientist.

Ku Klux Klan: secret society formed in the South following the Civil War to promote white supremacy

spirited: carried away secretly and swiftly

I was born in Diamond Grove, Mo., about the close of the great Civil War, in a little one-roomed log shanty, on the home of Mr. Moses Carver, a German by birth and the owner of my mother, my father being the property of Mr. Grant, who owned the adjoining plantation. I am told that my father was killed while hauling wood with an ox team. In some way he fell from the load, under the wagon. . . .

At the close of the war the **Ku Klux Klan** was at its height in that section of Missouri. My mother was stolen with myself, a wee babe in her arms. My brother James was grabbed and **spirited** away to the woods by Mr. Carver. He tried to get me, but could not. They carried my mother and myself down into Arkansas, and sold my mother. At that time I was nearly dead with the whooping cough that I had caught on the way. I was so very frail and sick that they thought of course that I would die within a few days. Mr. Carver immediately sent a very fine race horse and some money to purchase us back. The man (Bently by name) returned with the money and myself, having given the horse

---

1894

| 1894 Carver receives a bachelor's degree in agriculture. | 1896 Carver receives a master's degree in agriculture. He accepts a teaching position at Tuskegee Institute. | 1906 Carver begins a "school on wheels" for Alabama farmers to help them improve their farming methods. |

for me. The horse was valued at $300. Every effort was made to find my mother, but to no avail.

In the meantime my only two sisters died and were buried. My brother James and I grew up together, sharing each other's sorrows on the splendid farm owned by Mr. Carver. When just a mere tot in short **dresses** my very soul thirsted for an education. I literally lived in the woods. I wanted to know every strange stone, flower, insect, bird, or beast. No one could tell me.

My only book was an old Webster's Elementary Spelling Book. I would seek the answer here without satisfaction. I almost knew the book by heart. At the age of 19 years my brother left the old home for Fayetteville, Arkansas. Shortly after, at the age of 10 years, I left for Neosho, a little town just 8 miles from our farm, where I could go to school. Mr. and Mrs. Carver were perfectly willing for us to go where we could be educated the same as white children. I remained here about two years, got an opportunity to go to Fort Scott, Kansas with a family. They drove through the country.

Every year I went to school, supporting myself by cooking and doing all kinds of house work in private families. At the age of nineteen years I went back to see my brother and Mr. and Mrs. Carver. I had not improved much in **stature**, as I rode on a half-fare ticket. The conductor thought I was rather small to be traveling alone. I spent the summer here, and returned to Minneapolis, Kansas where I finished my high school work.

dresses: child's clothing

stature: size and height

Carver (second from right) assists a student in a chemistry laboratory at Tuskegee Institute where he served as head of the agriculture department.

1921 Carver gains national recognition for his research on peanuts.

1941 George Washington Carver Museum is dedicated at Tuskegee Institute.

77

minutia: (minutiae) details

liberally patroned: used a lot

prima dona: (prima donna) the main female singer

rehearse: tell in detail

invariably: always

matriculation: enrollment

c: (cents)

suet: fat

The sad news reached me here that James, my only brother, had died with the small pox. Being conscious as never before that I was left alone, I trusted God and pushed ahead. In working for others I had learned the **minutia** of laundering. I opened a laundry for myself; got all I could do.

After finishing high school here I made application to enter a certain College in Iowa. I was admitted, went but when the President saw I was colored he would not receive me. I had spent nearly all of my money, and had to open a laundry here. I was **liberally patroned** by the students. I remained here until spring and went to Winterset, Iowa, as first cook in a large hotel.

One evening I went to a white church, and set in the rear of the house. The next day a handsome man called for me at the hotel, and said his wife wanted to see me. When I reached the splendid residence I was astonished to recognize her as the **prima dona** in the choir. I was most astonished when she told me that my fine voice had attracted her. I had to sing quite a number of pieces for her, and agree to come to her house at least once a week; and from that time till now Mr. and Mrs. Milholland have been my warmest and most helpful friends.

I cooked at this hotel for some time; then opened a laundry for myself. I ran this laundry for one year. This same Mr. and Mrs. Milholland encouraged me to go to college. It was her custom to have me come at the day and **rehearse** to her the doings of the day. She would **invariably** laugh after such a recital and say, "Whoever heard of any one person doing half so many things."

She encouraged me to sing and paint, for which arts I had passionate fondness. In one years time I had saved sufficient money to take me to Simpson College, at Indianola, Iowa where I took art, music and college work. I open a laundry here for my support. After all my **matriculation** fees had been paid I had 10 **c** worth of corn meal, and the other 5 c I spent for beef **suet**. I lived on these two things one whole week—it took that

Tuskegee Institute was an all-black school in Alabama established in 1881. This photograph taken in 1902 shows a history class in progress.

Industrialist Henry Ford (right) gave Carver the funds to build a food research laboratory. Guests at the opening ceremony ate food that Carver had made from weeds and wild vegetables.

long for the people to learn that I wanted clothes to wash. After that week I had many friends and plenty of work.

I would never allow anyone to give me money, no difference how badly I needed it. I wanted literally to earn my living. I remained here for three years; then entered the Iowa State College, at Ames, Iowa, where I pursued my Agricultural work, taking two degrees, Bachelor and Master.

After finishing my Bachelor's degree I was elected a member of the faculty, and given charge of the greenhouse, bacteriological laboratory, and the laboratory work. . . .

Mr. Washington said he needed a man of my training. I accepted and came to **Tuskegee** nearly 27 years ago, and have been here ever since.

Mr. Washington:
Booker T. Washington, a great black American educator

Tuskegee:
Tuskegee Institute, a college in Alabama for black Americans, headed by Booker T. Washington

---

At the Tuskegee Institute Carver became especially well known for his experiments with peanuts. He created more than 300 products from peanuts. Carver also experimented with other plants that grew well in the southern soil. He worked closely with southern farmers, especially blacks, to teach them better farming methods. He was also greatly concerned with the improvement of race relations. Carver died in 1943.

Reprinted from *George Washington Carver: In His Own Words*, pp. 23–25, by Gary R. Kremer, by permission of the University of Missouri Press. Copyright © 1987 by the Curators of the University of Missouri.

The Jungle

" The hands of these men would be criss-crossed with cuts, until you could no longer pretend to count them or to trace them."

Upton Sinclair

Upton Sinclair was surprised by the public's strong reaction to his book *The Jungle*. Here he is shown with his son in 1905.

Jurgis: foreign-born worker in Chicago meat-packing plant

Jonas: Jurgis's friend

Durham's: name of the meat-packing plant

alchemists: chemists who worked with magic

tripe: stomach lining of an animal

suet: fat

waste ends: remains that are thrown away after butchering

hopper: container

grouse: a wild bird

In 1904 writer Upton Sinclair spent several weeks in the Chicago stockyards and meat-packing plants. Dressed in old clothes he went among the workers. Sinclair asked them about their work and the food products they made. He wrote of what he saw in a novel called *The Jungle*. Though a work of fiction, the book contained the true shocking details of food production in industrial America.

. . . One Sunday evening, **Jurgis** sat puffing his pipe by the kitchen stove, and talking with an old fellow whom **Jonas** had introduced, and who worked in the canning rooms at **Durham's**; and so Jurgis learned a few things about the great and only Durham canned goods, which had become a national institution. They were regular **alchemists** at Durham's; they advertised a mushroom catsup, and the men who made it did not know what a mushroom looked like. They advertised "potted chicken,"— and it was like the boarding-house soup of the comic papers, through which a chicken had walked. . . . Perhaps they had a secret process for making chickens chemically— who knows? said Jurgis's friends; the things that went into the mixture were **tripe**, and the fat of pork, and beef **suet**, and hearts of beef, and finally the **waste ends** of veal, when they had any. They put these up in several grades, and sold them at several prices; but the contents of the cans all came out of the same **hopper**. And then there was "potted game" and "potted **grouse**," "potted ham"

1856		
1856 Chicago becomes world's busiest railroad center.	**1865** Union Stock Yards begin operation in Chicago.	**1880** Refrigerated rail cars are in common use.

and "**devilled** ham"— **de-vyled**, as the men called it. "De-vyled" ham was made out of the waste ends of smoked beef that were too small to be sliced by the machines; and also tripe, dyed with chemicals so that it would not show white; and trimmings of hams and corned beef; and potatoes, skins and all; and finally the hard **cartilaginous gullets** of beef, after the tongues had been cut out. All this **ingenious** mixture was ground up and flavoured with spices to make it taste like something. Anybody who could invent a new imitation had been sure of a fortune from old Durham, said Jurgis's informant; but it was hard to think of anything new in a place where so many sharp wits had been at work for so long; where men welcomed **tuberculosis** in the cattle they were feeding, because it made them fatten more quickly; and where they bought up all the old **rancid** butter left over in the grocery stores of a continent, and "**oxidized**" it by a forced-air process, to take away the odour, rechurned it with skim-milk, and sold it in bricks in the cities! Up to a year or two ago it had been the custom to kill horses in the yards—**ostensibly** for fertilizer; but after long **agitation** the newspapers had been able to make the public realize that the horses were being canned. Now it was against the law to kill horses in **Packingtown**, and the law was really complied with—for the present, at any rate....

There was another interesting set of statistics that a person might have gathered in Packingtown—those of the various **afflictions** of the workers. When Jurgis had first inspected the packing plants with **Szedvilas**, he had marvelled while he listened to the tale of all the things that were made out of the **carcasses** of animals, and of all the lesser industries that were maintained there; now he found that each one of these lesser industries was a separate little **inferno**, in its way as horrible as the **killing beds**, the source and fountain

devilled: (deviled) chopped up fine and highly seasoned

de-vyled: a play on words meaning made very bad or very dirty

cartilaginous gullets: hard parts of the throat

ingenious: cleverly invented

tuberculosis: disease that infects the lungs

rancid: spoiled

oxidized: added oxygen to

ostensibly: supposedly

agitation: stirring up people to cause change

Packingtown: area of town where the meat-packing plants were located

afflictions: diseases; injuries

Szedvilas: foreign-born worker

carcasses: dead bodies

inferno: place of great suffering

killing beds: area where the animals are killed

Piles of frozen meat line the walls of this cold storage plant in Chicago's meat-packing district. In the early 1900s all the work in the plants was done by hand.

1898 Spoiled canned meat causes the death of many soldiers in the Spanish-American War.

1906 Sinclair publishes *The Jungle*. Congress passes legislation to regulate the food industry.

sceptical: (skeptical) doubtful; unsure

bore: carried

pickle rooms: areas where the meats are pickled, or preserved

Antanas: another worker

put him out of the world: kill him

floorsmen: men who supply materials to assembly-line workers

pulling hides: removing skins from the carcasses

quarters: after butchering, one-quarter bodies of beef

cars: railroad cars

rheumatism: disease that causes stiffness, swelling, or pain in the muscles or joints

of them all. The workers in each of them had their own peculiar diseases. And the wandering visitor might be **sceptical** about all the swindles, but he could not be sceptical about these, for the worker **bore** the evidence of them about on his own person—generally he had only to hold out his hand.

There were the men in the **pickle rooms**, for instance, where old **Antanas** had gotten his death; scarce a one of these that had not some spot of horror on his person. Let a man so much as scrape his finger pushing a truck in the pickle rooms, and he might have a sore that would **put him out of the world**; all the joints in his fingers might be eaten by the acid, one by one. Of the butchers and **floorsmen**, the beef-boners and trimmers, and all those who used knives, you could scarcely find a person who had the use of his thumb; time and time again the base of it had been slashed, till it was a mere lump of flesh against which the man pressed the knife to hold it. The hands of these men would be criss-crossed with cuts, until you could no longer pretend to count them or to trace them. They would have no nails—they had worn them off **pulling hides**; their knuckles were swollen so that their fingers spread out like a fan. There were men who worked in the cooking rooms, in the midst of steam and sickening odours, by artificial light; in these rooms the germs of tuberculosis might live for two years, but the supply was renewed every hour. There were the beef-luggers, who carried two-hundred-pound **quarters** into the refrigerator **cars**—a fearful kind of work, that began at four o'clock in the morning, and that wore out the most powerful men in a few years. There were those who worked in the chilling rooms, and whose special disease was **rheumatism**; the time limit that a man could work in the chilling rooms was said to be five years. There were the wool-pluckers, whose hands went to pieces even sooner than the hands of the pickle men; for the pelts of the sheep had to be painted with acid to loosen the wool, and then the pluckers had to pull out this wool with their bare hands, till the acid had eaten their fingers off. There were those who made the tins for the canned meat; and their hands, too, were a maze

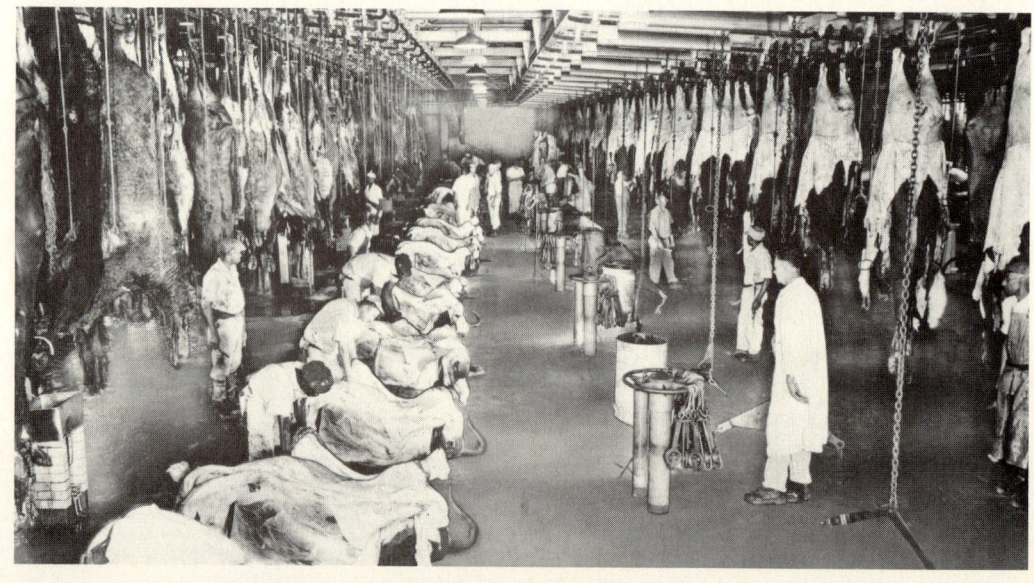

Meat-packing plants were forced to clean up their operations as a result of the reaction to Sinclair's book.

Before *The Jungle* was published, people who bought meat in markets such as this had no idea how the meat had been prepared.

of cuts, and each cut represented a chance for blood poisoning. Some worked at the **stamping machines**, and it was seldom that one could work long there at the pace that was set, and not give out and forget himself, and have a part of his hand chopped off. There were the "hoisters," as they were called, whose task it was to press the lever which lifted the dead cattle off the floor. They ran along upon a rafter, peering down through the damp and the steam; and as old Durham's architects had not built the killing room for the convenience of the hoisters, at every few feet they would have to stoop under a beam, say four feet above the one they ran on; which got them into the habit of stooping, so that in a few years they would be walking like chimpanzees. Worst of any, however, were the fertilizer-men, and those who served in the cooking rooms. These people could not be shown to the visitor, for the odour of a fertilizer-man would scare any ordinary visitor at a hundred yards; and as for the other men, who worked in tank rooms full of steam, and in some of which there were open **vats** near the level of the floor, their peculiar trouble was that they fell into the vats; and when they were fished out, there was never enough of them left to be worth exhibiting—sometimes they would be overlooked for days, till all but the bones of them had gone out to the world as Durham's Pure Leaf Lard!

stamping machines: machines used to form and shape metal cans

vats: large cooking pots

Readers of *The Jungle*, including President Theodore Roosevelt, were sickened by Upton Sinclair's portrait of conditions in the meat-packing industry. The book greatly influenced the passage of the Pure Food and Drug and Meat Inspection acts. These acts allowed Congress to begin regulation of the food industry.

From *The Jungle*, pp. 117–20, by Upton Sinclair. Copyright © 1905, 1906, 1933, 1946 by Upton Sinclair. All rights reserved. Reprinted by permission of Viking Penguin, a division of Penguin Books USA Inc.

UNIT 8

WORLD IN CRISIS

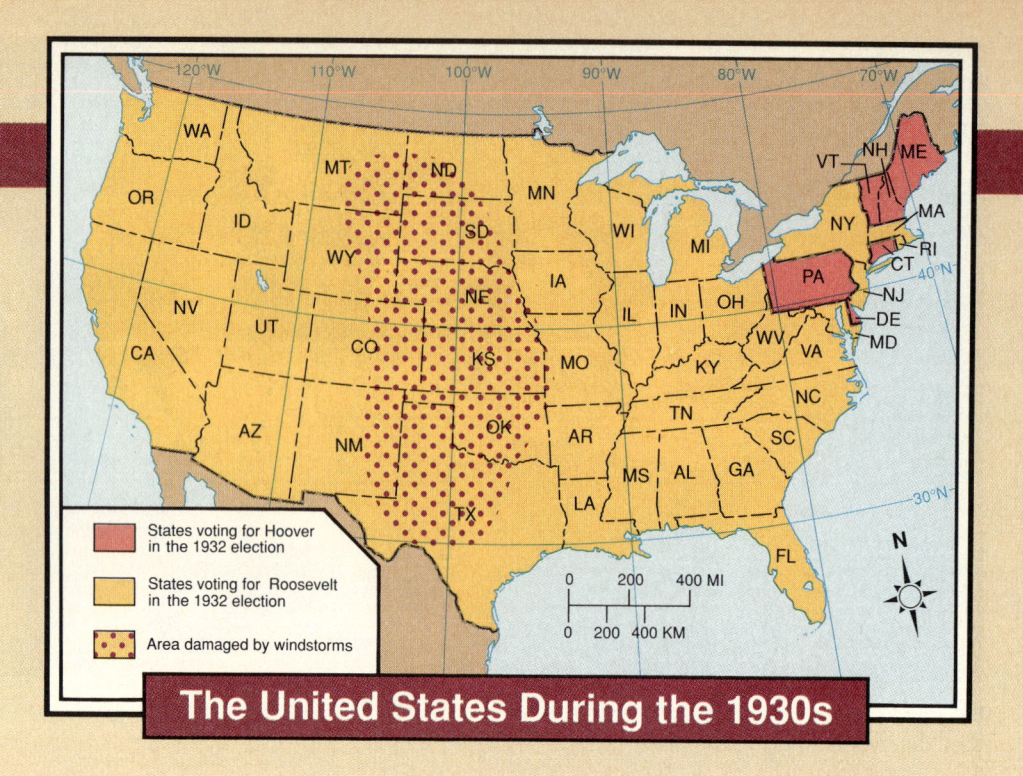

The United States During the 1930s

- States voting for Hoover in the 1932 election
- States voting for Roosevelt in the 1932 election
- Area damaged by windstorms

World War I was different from earlier wars. Soldiers lived and fought in trenches. Airplanes battled in the sky. The tank, the machine gun, and poison gas had devastating effects. Ten million soldiers were killed and over twenty million were wounded. Monarchies collapsed, and new nations emerged from old empires.

After the war the American economy boomed at first. New inventions such as radios, movies, automobiles, and refrigerators made life easier. By 1920 more people lived in cities than on farms. But living conditions for farmers and workers worsened during this same period. Wages and crop prices fell.

Hard times came for everyone after the stock market crashed in 1929. Banks cut loans to businesses, businesses cut production, and millions of workers lost their jobs. Spending dropped, businesses went bankrupt, and banks failed. Between 1933 and 1940 eight to thirteen million Americans were unemployed each year. It was the longest period of high unemployment in United States history.

A drought and destructive windstorms ruined thousands of farms in the Great Plains during the 1930s. Many farm families were forced to become **migrant workers.** The Great Depression also severely affected

migrant workers: people who move from place to place to find work

1915	1920	1925

■ **1918** Lieutenant Phelps Harding writes a letter after U.S. troops defeat the Germans at St. Mihiel in France.

the coal mines of West Virginia, already torn by strikes. Miners' wages were cut and many mines closed.

In 1932 Franklin Roosevelt ran for president promising Americans a **New Deal.** Once elected he quickly put into effect dozens of programs designed to help the needy, provide jobs, and reform business and government practices. For the first time the government became involved in areas such as economic regulation and social welfare. Roosevelt's New Deal helped but did not cure America's economic problems. Unemployment was still as high as 15 percent in 1940. Only America's entry into World War II and the need for war products created enough jobs to bring about full employment.

New Deal: programs for economic recovery and reform

As unemployment soared during the Great Depression, millions of Americans fell victim to poverty.

In this unit three people view the events of these critical years in America's history.

- **Lieutenant Phelps Harding** writes a letter home describing events in France toward the end of World War I.
- **Eleanor Roosevelt** describes in her autobiography the conditions she saw in a West Virginia coal-mining town.
- In an oral history **Peggy Terry** remembers her life as a migrant worker in the 1930s.

1930	1935	1940
	1933 Eleanor Roosevelt visits the coal-mining areas of West Virginia.	1938 Peggy Terry and her husband become migrant workers in the Rio Grande Valley.

The Push Forward

" I was surprised at the indifference I felt toward dead Americans...."
Lieutenant Phelps Harding

During World War I soldiers ate, slept, and fought in dirt ditches called trenches.

Allies: the nations that fought Germany in WWI

American Expeditionary Forces: soldiers sent to Europe by the U.S. Army

commenced: began

St. Mihiel: town in France

offensive: military attack

When World War I broke out in Europe in 1914, America remained neutral. But German attacks on unarmed ships in the Atlantic Ocean caused America to enter the war in 1917. The United States Navy helped the British overcome the German navy, and American soldiers helped to turn the war in favor of the **Allies.** A soldier with the **American Expeditionary Forces** writes a letter about events in France in 1918.

> 22 September, 1918.
> Dear Christine,
> My last letter was written just before we **commenced** the **St. Mihiel offensive**, which began September 12th. I am writing this letter in what was then German occupied territory, sixteen kilometers from our original front line.
> When the Division left the Chateau Thierry front we thought we were bound for a rest camp.... Then the order came to move. We marched by night and slept in the daytime.... Our stopping places at the end of each march were thick woods. It is no fun moving into thick, wet woods in the dark, and trying to find places to sleep.
> The last night the rain and wind were fierce—I had to be careful not to lose my platoon, the night was so dark and the marching conditions so

Apr. 1917		
Apr. 1917 America declares war on Germany and enters World War I.	**June 1917** America sends troops to France.	**June 1918** America helps France stop German troops near Paris.

bad. We moved to within about a kilometer of our line, my battalion being in support of the regiment, and took cover in an old drainage ditch. Wet? Rather!

At exactly 1 A.M., the artillery cut loose. It seemed as if all the artillery in France had suddenly opened up. . . . It was a wonderful and awe-inspiring sight.

At 5 A.M., the assault troops went over the top. We followed in the third wave. . . .

Before we had gone far prisoners began to come in first by twos and threes, then by platoons and companies. We took 13,000 **Boche** that day. We passed dead men of both armies, but many more Boche than Americans. I was surprised at the indifference I felt toward dead Americans—they seemed a perfectly natural thing to come across, and I felt absolutely no shudder go down my back as I would have had I seen the same thing a year ago.

Boche: Germans

We kept on going forward until we reached the crest of a hill, and here the shelling became so heavy that we made ourselves as small as possible in ditches and holes. Shells were striking all around us, and too close for comfort. . . .

After taking the shelling for possibly twenty minutes our artillery spotted the Boche batteries, which were either destroyed or withdrew, permitting us to move forward again. . . .

Just one more item before I end this letter and go to inspect my platoon. We had expected to be relieved before now, but yesterday news arrived that changed all our plans. Probably my battalion will go into the new line in a day or so, possibly to stay there for a fairly long period. We may even move forward again—no one knows definitely. Anyway, you may not hear from me for a couple of weeks or so—longer, if we push on toward **Berlin.**

Berlin: the capital of Germany in 1918

The American forces did push on, but they did not have to go all the way to Berlin. During this final offensive Allied troops proved their superiority. German leaders became convinced that they could not win against the Allies. On November 11, 1918, the Germans agreed to stop fighting. World War I was over.

From Lyn Macdonald, *1914–1918: Voices and Images of the Great War* (London: Michael Joseph Ltd., 1988), pp. 304–6. Copyright © Lyn Macdonald 1988. Reproduced by permission of Michael Joseph Ltd.

		Nov. 1918
Aug. 1918 Allies win the Second Battle of the Marne, marking the turning point of the war.	**Sept. 1918** Americans win at St. Mihiel. Harding writes this letter.	**Nov. 1918** World War I ends.

This I Remember

"I liked the theory of trying to put people to work to help themselves."
Eleanor Roosevelt

First Lady Eleanor Roosevelt (right front) went into the heart of a coal mine to observe the working conditions of miners.

polio: disease that can cause paralysis of the muscles

After Franklin Roosevelt was stricken with **polio,** Eleanor Roosevelt helped keep his political career alive. She often made fact-finding trips for him when he was governor of New York and later when he was president. She observed firsthand the people and conditions across the nation during the Great Depression. In her autobiography she recalls a visit to an experimental homestead community in 1933 in the coal-mining areas of West Virginia.

Quakers: members of the Society of Friends, a Christian religious group

company house: company-owned house where employees had to live

company store: company-run store where employees had to buy supplies

In the autumn I was invited by the **Quakers** to investigate the conditions that they were making an effort to remedy in the coal-mining areas of West Virginia. My husband agreed that it would be a good thing to do, so the visit was arranged. I had not been photographed often enough then to be recognized, so I was able to spend a whole day going about the area near Morgantown, West Virginia, without anyone's discovering who I was. . . .

In a **company house** I visited, where the people had evidently seen better days, the man showed me his weekly pay slips. A small amount had been deducted toward his bill at the **company store** and for his rent and for oil for his mine lamp. These deductions left him less than a dollar in cash each week. There were six children in the family, and they acted as though they were afraid of strangers. I noticed a bowl on the table filled with scraps, the kind that you or I might give to a dog, and I saw children . . . take a handful out of that bowl and go out munching. That was all they had to eat.

1921		
1921 Eleanor aids in her husband's political career after he contracts polio.	**1932** Franklin is elected president of the United States.	**1933** Eleanor becomes closely involved in the Great Depression recovery programs.

As I went out, two of the children had gathered enough courage to stand by the door, the little boy holding a white rabbit in his arms. It was evident that it was a most cherished pet. The little girl was thin and scrawny, and had a gleam in her eyes as she looked at her brother. She said, "He thinks we are not going to eat it, but we are," and at that the small boy fled down the road clutching the rabbit closer than ever.

It happened that **William C. Bullitt** was at dinner that night and I have always been grateful to him for the check he sent me the next day, saying he hoped it might help to keep the rabbit alive.

This trip to the mining areas was my first contact with the work being done by the Quakers. I liked the theory of trying to put people to work to help themselves. The men were started on projects and taught to use their abilities to develop new skills. The women were encouraged to revive any household arts they might once have known but which they had neglected in the drab life of the mining village.

This was only the first of many trips into the mining districts but it was the one that started the homestead idea. The University of West Virginia, in Morgantown, had already created a committee to help the miners on the Quaker agricultural project. . . . It was all experimental work, but it was designed to get people off **relief**, to put them to work building their own homes and to give them enough land to start growing food.

William C. Bullitt: then U.S. ambassador to France

relief: aid for the poor provided by a government agency

Eleanor focused much of her energy on human rights. She assisted in drawing up the Universal Declaration of Human Rights.

The "homestead" plan tried to place people in planned communities with homes, farms, and jobs. The plan was never very successful. But it helped expand Eleanor's **humanitarian** interests. She devoted much of her life to helping others in the United States and around the world. One of the most active and most loved first ladies, she was known as the "First Lady of the World."

humanitarian: concern for helping others

Excerpt from *The Autobiography of Eleanor Roosevelt*, pp. 177–78. Copyright © 1961 by Anna Eleanor Roosevelt. Reprinted by permission of Harper & Row, Publishers, Inc.

| 1935 Eleanor begins a daily newspaper column called "My Day." | 1939 Eleanor joins the National Association for the Advancement of Colored People (NAACP). | 1945 Eleanor is appointed a delegate to the United Nations. |

Hard Times

"Here were all these people living in old, rusted-out car bodies. I mean that was their home. There were people living in shacks made of orange crates...."

Peggy Terry

Too poor to own a car, two Arkansas cotton workers set out with their belongings in search of better jobs and wages in the West.

Low prices for farm products, the stock market crash in 1929, and the Great Depression were only some of the disasters endured by farmers in the 1920s and 1930s. A seven-year drought and destructive windstorms destroyed 50 million acres of land in the Great Plains. Many bankrupt farm families became **migrant workers** who followed the crop harvests. Peggy Terry describes her memories of life as a migrant worker in the 1930s.

migrant workers: people who move from place to place to find work

Rio Grande Valley: river valley in south Texas near the Mexican border

My husband and me were migrant workers. We went down in the valley of Texas, which is very beautiful. We picked oranges and lemons and grapefruits, limes in the **Rio Grande Valley**.

We got a nickel a bushel for citrus fruits. On the grapefruits you had to ring them. You hold a ring in your hand.... You climb the tree and you put that ring around the grapefruit. If the grapefruit slips through, you can't pick it.... You can work real hard, especially if you want to make enough to buy food that day—you'll pick some that aren't big enough. Then when you carry your box up and they check it, they throw out all the ones that go through the ring....

This may sound impossible, but if there's one thing that started me thinking, it was President Roosevelt's cuff links. I read in the paper how many pairs of cuff links he had. It told that some of them were rubies and precious stones—these were his cuff links. And I'll never forget, I was setting on an old tire out in the front yard and we were poor and hungry.

1920			1938
1920 Prices of farm products fall dramatically and remain low. Other businesses prosper.	**1929** The stock market crashes. Many banks and businesses are forced to close. The Great Depression begins.		**1938** Thousands of farm families are bankrupt. Peggy Terry becomes a migrant worker.

A South Dakota farmer watches as thousands of grasshoppers swarm on his land. After millions of acres had been destroyed by drought, there was little left for the grasshoppers to damage.

I was sitting out there in the hot sun, there weren't any trees. And I was wondering why it is that one man could have all those cuff links when we couldn't even have enough to eat. When we lived on gravy and biscuits. That's the first time I remember ever wondering why.

And when my father finally got his bonus, he bought a secondhand car for us to come back to Kentucky in. My dad said to us kids: "All of you get in the car. I want to take you and show you something." On the way over there, he'd talk about how life had been rough for us, and he said: "If you think it's been rough for us, I want you to see people that really had it rough." This was in Oklahoma City, and he took us to one of the **Hoovervilles**, and that was the most incredible thing.

Here were all these people living in old, rusted-out car bodies.

Hoovervilles: groups of shacks where homeless people lived; named after President Hoover because he failed to end the depression

Cyclones of choking black dust swept across the Great Plains in the mid 1930s. A severe drought and over-farming of the land turned the topsoil into dust. The area became known as the Dust Bowl.

91

Many families were forced to live in one-room shacks pieced together from scrap tin or cardboard boxes. Until President Roosevelt took office in 1933, there was no federal aid for the poor and homeless.

At least 13 million workers lost their jobs during the Great Depression. Without salaries people could not afford food or housing. The mood was summed up in a popular song called "Brother, Can You Spare a Dime?"

Central Park in New York City was home to hundreds of people who could no longer afford to pay rent. Small huts provided some protection from the cold winters.

Hundreds of sharecroppers were forced to leave southern farms as prices for crops hit rock bottom. Some lived in makeshift camps and shared the little food they had as they looked for other jobs.

I mean that was their home. There were people living in shacks made of orange crates. One family with a whole lot of kids were living in a piano box. This wasn't just a little section, this was maybe ten-miles wide and ten-miles long. People living in whatever they could junk together.

And when I read **Grapes of Wrath**—she bought that for me (indicates young girl seated across the room)—that was like reliving my life. Particularly the part where they lived in this Government camp. Because when we were picking fruit in Texas, we lived in a Government place like that. They came around, and they helped the women make mattresses. . . . And they showed us how to sew and make dresses. And every Saturday night, we'd have a dance. And when I was reading Grapes of Wrath . . . I was never so proud of poor people before, as I was after I read that book.

Grapes of Wrath: 1939 novel by John Steinbeck about the hardships suffered by migrant workers in the 1930s

During the Great Depression banks failed, and businesses went bankrupt. People lost their jobs, savings, and homes. Many turned to bread lines and soup kitchens run by charities to get food. They lived in shacks of tin and wood or roamed the country looking for work. Although Roosevelt's economic programs helped, only the mass production brought on by World War II finally conquered the severe unemployment.

From *Hard Times: An Oral History of the Great Depression*, pp. 49–50, by Studs Terkel. Copyright © 1970 by Studs Terkel. Reprinted by permission of Pantheon Books, a division of Random House, Inc.

UNIT 9

ALLIES IN ARMS

Europe in World War II

Allied Powers: the United States, Great Britain, China, the Soviet Union, and 46 other countries

Axis Powers: Germany, Italy, Japan, and six other countries

The war that raged throughout Europe and Asia finally came home to America on December 7, 1941 at Pearl Harbor in Hawaii. The surprise attack left almost 2,500 Americans dead. On December 8 the United States declared war on Japan and joined the other **Allied Powers** in the long struggle against the **Axis Powers**.

Fifteen million men left their families, homes, and jobs to join the fight first against Japan and then Germany. As the nation scrambled to produce the needed weapons, the women of America filled the gaps in factories left by the departing men. Three million women entered the work force during the war. Many of them went to work in factories, where they helped build tanks, airplanes, and weapons for the war effort. The number of women in the aircraft industry alone increased from 4,000 in pre-war factories to 360,000 during the war.

In Europe the Allied Powers planned an invasion of German-held France. Nearly 150,000 soldiers prepared for the bloody confrontation on June 6, 1944, when thousands of ships ferried Allied troops across the English Channel to reclaim the beaches at Normandy, France.

1941	1942
	■ 1942 Charlcia Neuman and millions of other women go to work for the war effort.

By the end of that day 10,000 Allied soldiers lay dead in the tides off Normandy's coast. But the Germans withdrew, finally giving the Allies an 80-square-mile entryway to Europe.

As the Allied troops advanced, they discovered the first of many concentration camps. Even though these soldiers had witnessed much death and destruction during this long war, they were horrified by the devastation they witnessed as they freed the skeletal survivors at Auschwitz and Belsen, Buchenwald and Dachau. Of the millions sent to the camps, only thousands lived to cheer the liberating soldiers. Nearly 11 million people died in the concentration camps, and the whole world grieved.

During World War II American soldiers in armored vehicles swept through France in pursuit of the Germans.

This unit contains the experiences of three individuals at home and abroad during World War II.

- **Charlcia Neuman** explains how her life changed when she became a riveter in a plant that produced fighter planes for the Army Air Force.
- **Ernie Pyle** writes a news article describing the terrible loss of life and materials in Normandy, France.
- The liberation of a concentration camp is described by **Colonel Walter J. Fellenz,** who helped free survivors of Dachau.

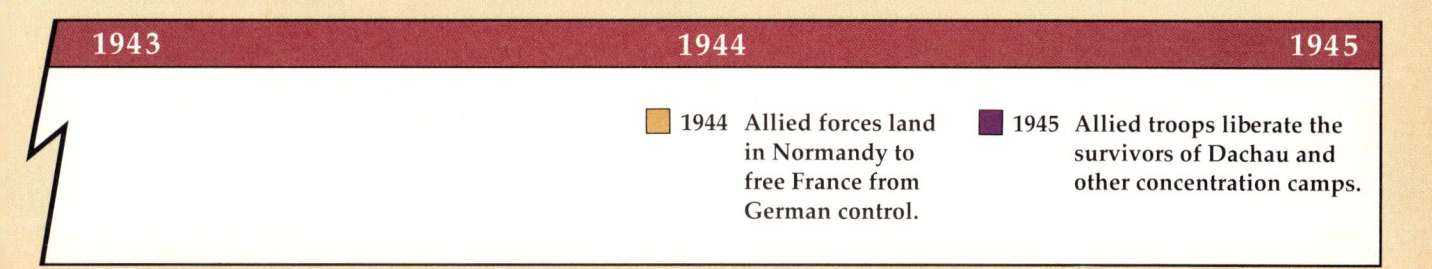

1943	1944	1945
	1944 Allied forces land in Normandy to free France from German control.	1945 Allied troops liberate the survivors of Dachau and other concentration camps.

Women in the War Effort

" It was mostly women on these jobs. "
Charlcia Neuman

During World War II women took over many of the factory jobs that had previously been held by men.

After the United States entered World War II in 1941, factories were built to produce the enormous amount of war materials needed for victory. However, as millions of men left for combat, factory workers became scarce, and the government began to recruit women to work. Millions of women responded. Charlcia Neuman recalls her experiences working in an aircraft factory in California.

reserves: the part of the armed forces not on active duty but which can be called upon in an emergency

Terminal Island: in Los Angeles

defense work: job that helped the war effort

Pearl Harbor. I remember that very definitely. I was standing at the sink. The man next door, he was a captain in the **reserves**. I remember opening the window and calling to him and telling him to go in and turn the radio on. I didn't like it, naturally —no one did—they came in with no warning at all and bombed Pearl Harbor. It was a terrible thing.

The patriotic feeling was so strong that anyone would have done anything to help. You never had any of this protest type of thing. There were a great many things that were wrong, especially what they did to the Japanese people that lived here. I knew one family that because the grandmother was Japanese, they had to leave their home. This was terrible. On the other hand, my husband had worked on **Terminal Island** in the schools there and amongst those people there were Japanese that were spies. Because of that, everybody suffered and it was wrong.

I started **defense work** in '42. I think a lot of it was because one of my neighbors found out about it, and she wanted me to go with her. I thought, "Well, now, this would take care of the situation." I still was getting along

1941

| 1941 The United States enters World War II. Fifteen million women are in the work force. | 1942 Government recruits women to work in defense plants. Neuman begins working in a plant. | 1943 The United States becomes the leading producer of aircraft in the world. |

on next to nothing; it was still difficult. And my husband was talking about whether he should quit the school board or not. In those days, they didn't belong to any union, and they were paid a very small amount. As prices were going up it wasn't enough to cover our expenses. So I said, "No, I'll go see what I can do."

My husband didn't like it. He was one of these men that never wanted his wife to work. He was German and was brought up with the idea that the man made the living; the woman didn't do that. But he found that it was a pretty good idea at the time. It was a necessity, because he would have had to do something else. We couldn't live on what he was making, so that's the way it goes.

And my brother, especially my youngest brother, he thought it was terrible. . . .

So, my family thought I was a little off for doing it. But if that's what I wanted to do, that's what I did. And my husband got used to the fact that his wife worked.

I went over and took tests to see about getting a job at **Vultee**. When I took the test, as far as using the hands and the eye and hand movements, I passed just about the highest. See, anything using my hands—I could take a little hand drill and go up and down these holes as fast as you could move, just go like that, where most people would break a drill. It was a very simple thing. The **riveting** is the same way. It's just a matter of rhythm. So it was easy to do.

Vultee: California defense plant that manufactured aircraft

riveting: fastening objects with metal bolts or pins

Women helped to maintain the trains used to ship soldiers and war materials across the United States.

1944 One in three women defense workers is a former full-time homemaker.

1945 World War II ends. Nineteen million women are in the work force.

1945

97

The United States was not the only country in World War II that had a shortage of male workers. Here English women break for tea while working on armored vehicles.

Downey: California manufacturing plant

jigs: devices for guiding a tool

ribs: short pieces that lie across and give shape to the wing of an airplane

P-38: fighter plane used in World War II

WACS: Women's Army Corps

break the color line: be the only minority member in a social situation

They had a school set up in **Downey** to show us how to do assembly work and riveting and the reasons for things—what was a good rivet and what wasn't. We went there about two weeks before we started to work. It was mostly women on these jobs. See, so many young men were in the service that it didn't leave very many of them to do these types of jobs; the ones that were kept out of the service could do the more specialized work. They had to have men to make these **jigs** and to make the forms for the **ribs**. That was beyond us.

I was started on this jig. The **P-38** that Lockheed put out was a twin engine, and we worked on the center part between the two hulls. It was a much heavier rivet that went into this. It was what they call cold riveting; you took them out of the icebox real cold and riveted it. That was harder work. . . .

Sometimes I had someone working with me and that made it a little faster, because otherwise I'd have to reach to the back and be sure it's in place. The person in the back would drill and you'd drill in the front, and then they'd be there all ready to rivet. My partner was better . . . than I was. She could hold it steadier. I wasn't strong enough. You had to hold that square bar on the other side while the gun was shooting on this side. It was quite a force on it. It was hard to do. . . .

Vultee was the first plant of this type in the area to hire a black girl. She was a very nice person. Wilhelmina was her first name, but I can't remember her last name. Her mother was a schoolteacher and she was from Los Angeles.

The girls that worked together became quite friendly. If someone happened to quit and went in the **WACS**, we would have a party. I remember this one time, we thought, "No, we're not going to have it at the restaurant; we'll have it in one of our homes and ask Willie to come, too." We didn't want to leave her out. About seven o'clock that night, we got a telegram from Willie saying she was so sorry she couldn't come, but that she appreciated us asking her. She didn't want to **break the color line**, but those things wouldn't happen anymore today.

But she was among the first blacks in our department. In that three years that I was there, then they began coming from the South. You could really tell the difference. The ones coming from the South were shy. It was very hard for them to mix with people. It was a very hard situation for them, but they were treated nice. . . .

Then there were the Mexican girls. They were treated just like we were. . . . They were very nice. They couldn't pronounce my name, and they always called me Charli. I remember this one, when I would walk up toward them, she would say, "Now you speak English; you know Charli can't speak Spanish." This one particular group was clustered in that area, but there were others scattered through the plant. It wasn't that they were separating this group; it just happened. I couldn't see that they were being **discriminated against** in any way. But at that time, the Negroes were just treated very badly. Here again, I've always been different, where things like this was concerned. I could see the wrong.

But the women on my crew were a bit like me. One girl lived in **San Pedro**. I think her folks were fishermen down there. And another one lived over in **Huntington Park**, just a plain ordinary family. At thirty-one, thirty-two, I was considered fairly old. There was one woman that I think was forty-eight when they hired her, and she was an old lady! But these girls were mostly younger; they were in their early twenties. I don't think any of them had children.

We kept pretty busy working all the time, and there wasn't much personal talk. We sat down as a group at lunchtime, though. We would just find some spot to sit and eat and talk about different things. We didn't have any close connections, so there wasn't very much that we could talk about. I just knew where they lived.

In the Los Angeles aircraft factories women made up more than 40 percent of the work force.

discriminated against: treated differently because of their race

San Pedro: in Los Angeles

Huntington Park: town southeast of Los Angeles

The number of women in the work force increased from about 15 million in 1941 to 19 million in 1945. Many of these women filled jobs once held by men, and they gained a new sense of independence. A poll taken in 1944 revealed that 75 percent of working women wanted to continue to work at their present jobs after the war. However, as the war ended, defense plants laid off millions, forcing many women back into more traditional jobs.

From Sherna Berger Gluck, *Rosie the Riveter Revisited* (New York: New American Library, 1988), pp. 163–66. Originally published by Twayne Publishers, 1985. Copyright © 1985 Sherna Berger Gluck. Reprinted by permission of Sherna Berger Gluck.

Normandy Invasion

"Men were sleeping on the sand, some of them sleeping forever."

Ernie Pyle

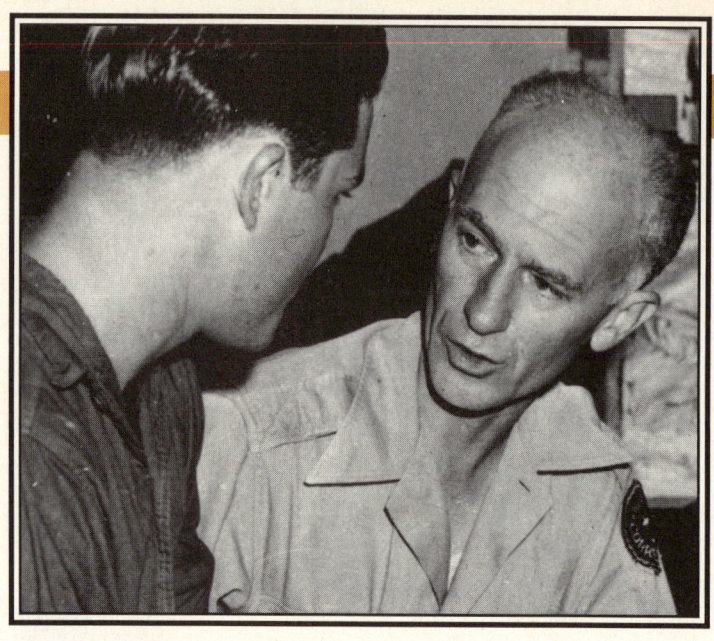

Ernie Pyle spent much of his time talking with and writing about the common soldiers in World War II.

The Allied invasion of Normandy on June 6, 1944, also known as D-day, was the largest invasion by sea in history and marked the turning point of World War II. Ernie Pyle was one of 28 correspondents with the United States troops in Normandy. His sensitive and sympathetic news stories about the ordinary soldier attracted millions of readers. Pyle won a Pulitzer Prize in 1944 for his coverage of World War II.

The Horrible Waste of War

beachhead: an area controlled by troops that have invaded an enemy shore

Normandy **Beachhead**
June 16, 1944

I took a walk along the historic coast of Normandy in the country of France.

It was a lovely day for strolling along the seashore. Men were sleeping on the sand, some of them sleeping forever. Men were floating in the water, but they didn't know they were in the water, for they were dead.

The water was full of squishy little jellyfish about the size of your hand. Millions of them. In the center each of them had a green design exactly like a four-leaf clover. The good-luck emblem. Sure. . . .

I walked for a mile and a half along the water's edge of our many-miled invasion beach. You wanted to walk slowly, for the detail on that beach was infinite.

The wreckage was vast and startling. The awful waste and destruction of war, even aside from the loss of human life, has always been one of its outstanding features

---

Dec. 1941

| Dec. 1941 | United States enters World War II. | Jan. 1943 | Allied leaders plan invasion of Europe. | Sept. 1943 | Italy surrenders to the Allies. |

to those who are in it. Anything and everything is **expendable**. And we did expend on our beachhead in Normandy during those first few hours.

* * *

For a mile out from the beach there were scores of tanks and trucks and boats that you could no longer see, for they were at the bottom of the water—swamped by overloading, or hit by shells, or sunk by mines. Most of their crews were lost.

You could see trucks tipped half over and swamped. You could see partly sunken barges, and the angled-up corners of jeeps, and small landing craft half submerged. And at low tide you could still see those vicious six-pronged iron **snares** that helped snag and wreck them.

On the beach itself, high and dry, were all kinds of wrecked vehicles. There were tanks that had only just made the beach before being knocked out. There were jeeps that had burned to a dull gray. There were big **derricks** on **caterpillar treads** that didn't quite make it. There were **half-tracks** carrying office equipment that had been made into a **shambles** by a single shell hit, their interiors still holding their useless **equipage** of smashed typewriters, telephones, office files.

There were **LCT's** turned completely upside down, and lying on their backs, and how they got that way I don't know. There were boats stacked on top of each other, their sides caved in, their suspension doors knocked off.

In this shoreline museum of **carnage** there were abandoned rolls of barbed wire and smashed bulldozers and big stacks of thrown-away lifebelts and piles of shells still waiting to be moved.

In the water floated empty life rafts and soldiers' packs and ration boxes, and mysterious oranges.

On the beach lay snarled rolls of telephone wire and big rolls of

expendable: worth sacrificing

snares: traps

derricks: machines for lifting and moving heavy objects

caterpillar treads: hinged metal strips that move a vehicle along the ground

half-tracks: vehicles with wheels in front and caterpillar treads in back

shambles: mess

equipage: equipment

LCT's: landing craft tanks

carnage: killing of many people

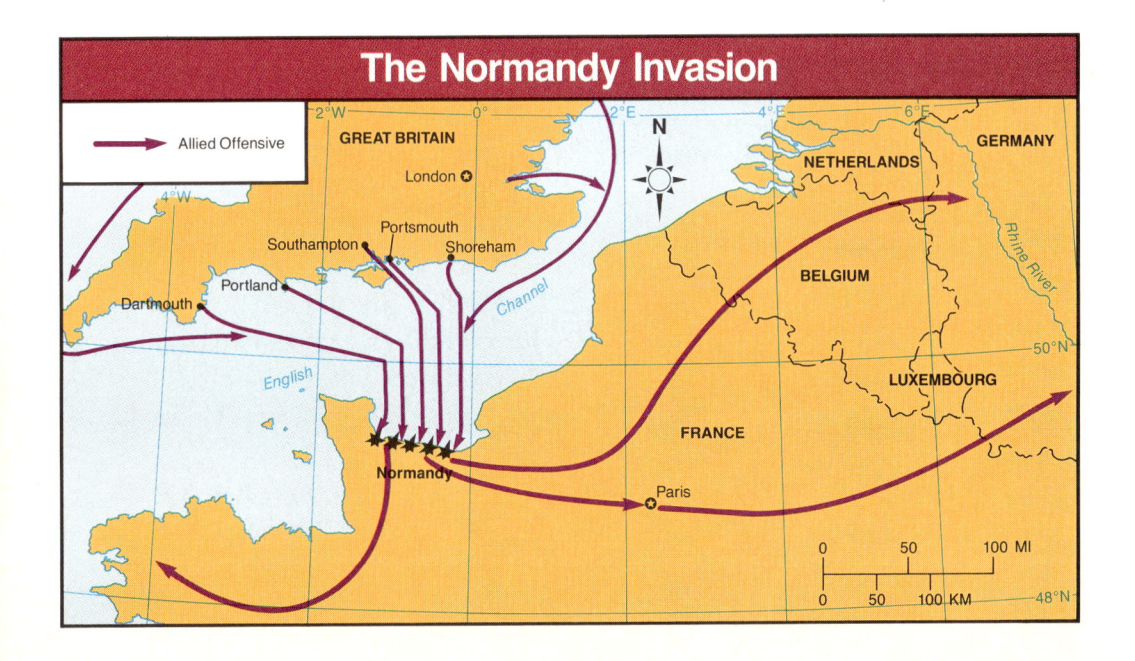

The Normandy Invasion

| June 1944 Allied forces invade Western Europe at Normandy, France. | Aug. 1944 Allies liberate Paris from German occupation. | May 1945 Allies move into Germany. Germany surrenders. The war in Europe is over. |

American reinforcements land at Normandy. Within ten days of D-day the Allies had landed some 557,000 soldiers and 81,000 vehicles on the beaches.

expended: sacrificed

toehold: entry position

conceive of: imagine

armada: fleet of warships

doughboys: soldiers with the United States infantry

tommy guns: Thompson submachine guns

compatriots: citizens of the same country

steel matting and stacks of broken, rusting rifles.

On the beach lay, **expended,** sufficient men and mechanism for a small war. They were gone forever now. And yet we could afford it.

We could afford it because we were on, we had our **toehold**, and behind us there were such enormous replacements for this wreckage on the beach that you could hardly **conceive of** their sum total. Men and equipment were flowing from England in such a gigantic stream that it made the waste on the beachhead seem like nothing at all, really nothing at all.

* * *

A few hundred yards back on the beach is a high bluff. Up there we had a tent hospital, and a barbed-wire enclosure for prisoners of war. From up there you could see far up and down the beach, in a spectacular crow's-nest view, and far out to sea.

And standing out there on the water beyond all this wreckage was the greatest **armada** man has ever seen. You simply could not believe the gigantic collection of ships that lay out there waiting to unload.

Looking from the bluff, it lay thick and clear to the far horizon of the sea and on beyond, and it spread out to the sides and was miles wide. Its utter enormity would move the hardest man.

As I stood up there I noticed a group of freshly taken German prisoners standing nearby. They had not yet been put in the prison cage. They were just standing there, a couple of **doughboys** leisurely guarding them with **tommy guns**.

The prisoners too were looking out to sea—the same bit of sea that for months and years had been so safely empty before their gaze. Now they stood staring almost as if in a trance.

They didn't say a word to each other. They didn't need to. The expression on their faces was something forever unforgettable. In it was the final horrified acceptance of their doom.

If only all Germans could have had the rich experience of standing on the bluff and looking out across the water and seeing what their **compatriots** saw.

A Long Thin Line of Personal Anguish

Normandy Beachhead
June 17, 1944

In the **preceding** column we told about the D-day wreckage among our machines of war that were expended in taking one of the Normandy beaches.

But there is another and more human litter. It extends in a thin little line, just like a high-water mark, for miles along the beach. This is the **strewn** personal gear, gear that will never be needed again, of those who fought and died to give us our entrance into Europe.

Here in a jumbled row for mile on mile are soldiers' packs. Here are socks and shoe polish, sewing kits, diaries, Bibles and hand grenades. Here are the latest letters from home, with the address on each one neatly **razored out**—one of the security precautions enforced before the boys **embarked**.

Here are toothbrushes and razors, and snapshots of families back home staring up at you from the sand. Here are pocketbooks, metal mirrors, extra trousers, and bloody, abandoned shoes. Here are broken-handled shovels, and portable radios smashed almost beyond recognition. . . .

Here are torn pistol belts and canvas water buckets, first-aid kits and jumbled heaps of lifebelts. I picked up a pocket Bible with a soldier's name in it, and put it in my jacket. I carried it half a mile or so and then put it back down on the beach. I don't know why I picked it up, or why I put it back down.

Soldiers carry strange things ashore with them. In every invasion you'll find at least one soldier hitting the beach at **H-hour** with a banjo slung over his shoulder. The most **ironic** piece of equipment marking

preceding: one that came before

strewn: scattered

razored out: cut out with a razor

embarked: started out

H-hour: military term for time at which operation will begin

ironic: opposite of what might be expected; showing great contrast

On the day of the invasion German defenders were surprised by Allied tanks that had been specially adapted to float ashore.

103

American troops move onto the beach at Normandy. The balloons, tied to the ground with cables, were used to stop low-level attacks by enemy planes.

dominant: main

in vain: without success

anguish: great suffering

our beach—this beach of first despair, then victory—is a tennis racket that some soldier had brought along. It lies lonesomely on the sand, clamped in its rack, not a string broken.

Two of the most **dominant** items in the beach refuse are cigarets and writing paper. Each soldier was issued a carton of cigarets just before he started. Today these cartons by the thousand, watersoaked and spilled out, mark the line of our first savage blow.

Writing paper and air-mail envelopes come second. The boys had intended to do a lot of writing in France. Letters that would have filled those blank, abandoned pages.

Always there are dogs in every invasion. There is a dog still on the beach today, still pitifully looking for his masters.

He stays at the water's edge, near a boat that lies twisted and half sunk at the water line. He barks appealingly to every soldier who approaches, trots eagerly along with him for a few feet, and then, sensing himself unwanted in all this haste, runs back to wait **in vain** for his own people at his own empty boat.

* * *

Over and around this long thin line of personal **anguish**, fresh men today are rushing vast supplies to keep our armies pushing on into France. Other squads of men pick amidst the wreckage to salvage ammunition and equipment that are still usable.

Men worked and slept on the beach for days before the last D-day victim was taken away for burial.

I stepped over the form of one youngster whom I thought dead. But when I looked down I saw he was only sleeping.... He lay on one elbow, his hand suspended in the air about six inches from the ground. And in the palm of his hand he held a large, smooth rock.

I stood and looked at him a long time. He seemed in his sleep to hold that rock lovingly, as though it were his last link with a vanishing world. I have no idea at all why he went to sleep with the rock in his hand, or what kept him from dropping it once he was asleep. It was just one of those little things without explanation that a person remembers for a long time.

* * *

The strong, swirling tides of the Normandy coastline shift the **contours** of the sandy beach as they move in and out. They carry soldiers' bodies out to sea, and later they return them. They cover the corpses of heroes with sand, and then **in their whims** they uncover them.

As I plowed out over the wet sand of the beach on that first day ashore, I walked around what seemed to be a couple of pieces of driftwood sticking out of the sand. But they weren't driftwood.

They were a soldier's two feet. He was completely covered by the shifting sands except for his feet. The toes of his GI shoes pointed toward the land he had come so far to see, and which he saw so briefly.

contours: outlines

in their whims: for no apparent reason

Although the beaches at Normandy were covered with bodies, the casualties were much lower than expected. Fewer than 2,500 Allied soldiers lost their lives on D-day.

Within a few months of D-day Allied troops had forced the German army out of France. Ernie Pyle's next assignment as a journalist was to cover the fighting in the Pacific, since his **dispatches** from Europe about the ordinary soldiers had raised the morale of Americans everywhere. Pyle was killed by a sniper on Ie Shima, a tiny island near Okinawa in the Pacific, on April 18, 1945.

dispatches: news stories

From *Ernie's War*, ed. David Nichols (New York: Random House, 1986), pp. 280–84. Reprinted by permission of Scripps Howard Foundation.

Impressions of Dachau

❝ This was an organized scheme of destruction of a whole race of people! ❞
Colonel Walter J. Fellenz

More than 30,000 prisoners are believed to have died at Dachau. The dead were burned in cremation ovens like those shown above.

On April 29, 1945, Colonel Walter J. Fellenz met with the commander of another battalion about 15 miles northwest of Munich, Germany. Colonel Fellenz did not realize that the meeting place was the concentration camp at Dachau. There he was to join those who liberated the prisoners. Nothing in their experience prepared the troops for what they found that day.

finishing school: private school that prepares young women for social life rather than for a career

SS: Schutzstaffel; elite police and military unit of the Nazi Party that served Hitler

Nearly a thousand yards from the rail siding was the camp itself. The approach was a wide, two-lane road with a lawn down the middle. One could imagine from the impressive massiveness of the gray administrative buildings and barracks, the fine lawns, great walls and black, iron-grilled gates that you were approaching a wealthy girls **finishing school** in the suburbs of one of our great cities. All was neat, orderly, efficient. . . .

At the main gate I met Brigadier General Linden, Lt. Col. Bolduc, and several staff officers and bodyguards. General Linden was waiting for a report from his aide who had been dispatched inside the camp to see if the camp had been deserted by the guards. Shortly after my arrival the aide reported that the **SS** had apparently deserted the camp. In we went, fully prepared to fight, however.

Several hundred yards inside the main gate we encountered the concentration enclosure itself. There before us, behind an electrically charged, barbed wire fence, stood a mass of cheering, half mad men,

1933

1933 Nazis set up a concentration camp in Dachau for political opponents and Jews.

1939 Nazis have built six concentrations camps.

women and children waving and shouting with happiness—their liberators had come! The noise was beyond comprehension! Every individual (over 32,000) who could utter a sound was cheering. Our hearts wept as we saw the tears of happiness fall from their cheeks. . . .

First I was led to the execution grounds, a small plot of ground, entirely enclosed by a hedge. There, I saw a mound of earth, about thirty feet long and four feet high. Here prisoners, six at a time were lined up, required to kneel down facing the mound, while the SS **nonchalantly** murdered them by shooting them in the back of the head from a range of two or three feet. The mound of earth was still wet with blood. Many thousands of men, women and children had been killed on this very plot of ground.

Next I was led to the storage warehouse. This large building contained the naked, dead bodies of over 4000 men, women and children, thrown one on top of the other like sacks of potatoes. The odor was terrific. . . . It was the most revolting smell I have ever experienced. . . .

You look at this unfair death, . . . and then you figure out how could people do this? How could they live with themselves? You could be brainwashed, death became something common. But this kind of death was not the common type. This was an organized scheme of destruction of a whole race of people!

nonchalantly: casually; without concern

About 160,000 people were imprisoned at Dachau's main camp. This photo was taken in 1945 when 32,000 prisoners were freed.

As other concentration camps were liberated, the Allies discovered the cruelty of the Nazis and learned of the millions of prisoners who were killed. Most of the dead and imprisoned were in the camps for no reason other than that they were Jews or had helped Jews. This persecution and murder of Jews has come to be known as the Holocaust. After the war the Allied Powers tried Nazi war criminals for their crimes against humanity during World War II.

From *The Liberators*, ed. Yaffa Eliach and Brana Gurewitsch (Brooklyn, NY: Center for Holocaust Studies Documentation and Research, 1981), pp. 36–37. Reprinted by permission of the publisher.

| 1942 Nazis decide to rid Europe of all Jews. | 1945 Allies liberate Dachau and other concentration camps. | 1949 More than 200 Nazi war criminals have been tried in Nuremberg Trials. |

UNIT 10

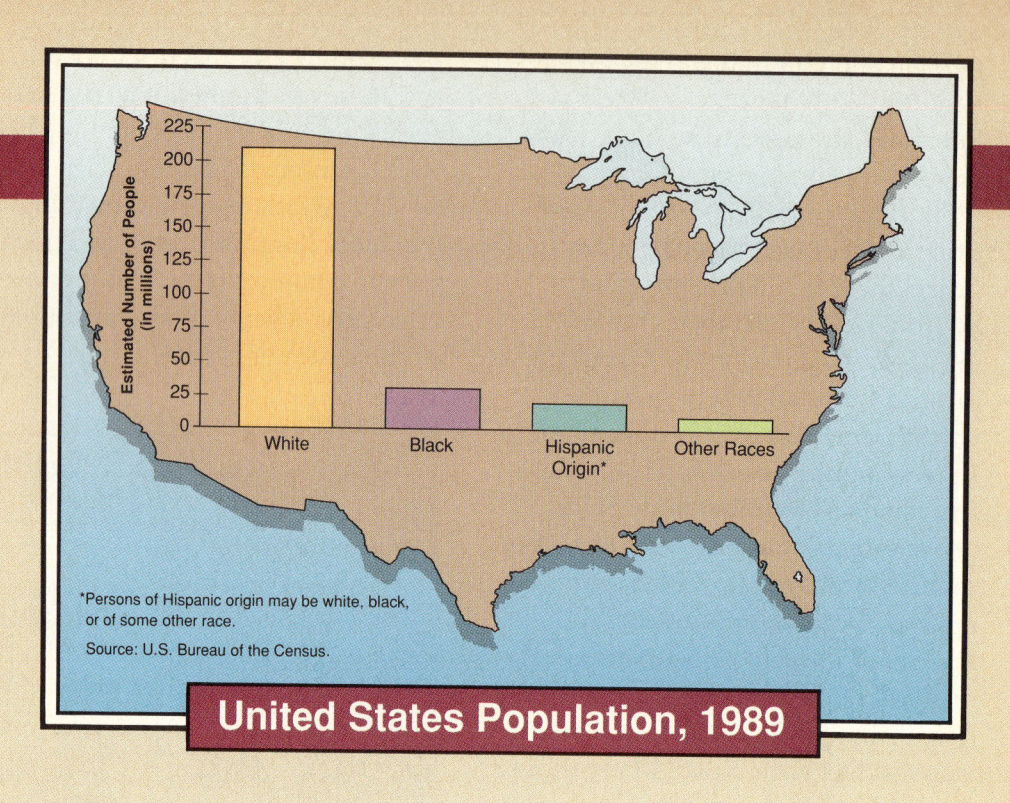

United States Population, 1989

*Persons of Hispanic origin may be white, black, or of some other race.

Source: U.S. Bureau of the Census.

---

segregated: separated by race

civil rights: rights guaranteed by the Constitution

boycotts: refusal to deal with a person or group as a way to protest

civil disobedience: opposing a policy or law by refusing to comply with it

discrimination: the act of showing prejudice by treating in a less favorable way

The years following World War II were marked by great prosperity for many Americans. Jobs were easy to find. The demand for consumer goods such as televisions, washing machines, and vacuum cleaners soared. Families grew at such a rate that the 1950s became known as the beginning of the "baby boom."

Several groups of Americans did not share in this prosperity. Most black Americans were still restricted to **segregated** communities, services, and schools. A powerful **civil rights** movement began to take shape. In 1954 the Supreme Court ruled that public schools could no longer be segregated. When the new ruling was not enforced in all areas, black Americans throughout the nation took part in marches, **boycotts,** and other acts of nonviolent **civil disobedience** to try to end the **discrimination**.

"Long Live the Cause!" was the motto adopted by another group of Americans who struggled against discrimination—migrant farm workers. Most of these workers were Hispanic Americans who lived in extreme poverty. In the 1960s migrant workers joined together to work for better working and living conditions. They formed a union that

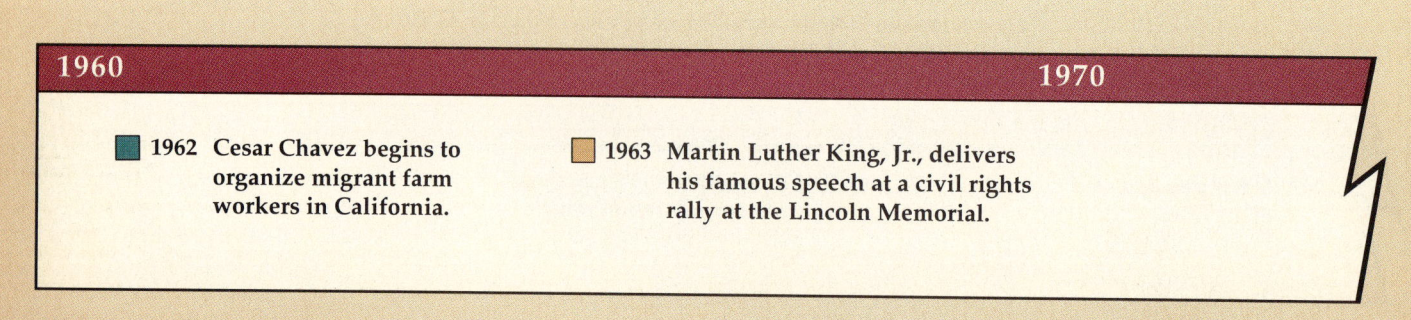

1960 | **1970**

■ **1962** Cesar Chavez begins to organize migrant farm workers in California.

■ **1963** Martin Luther King, Jr., delivers his famous speech at a civil rights rally at the Lincoln Memorial.

sponsored, among other things, a national boycott of California grapes. Their actions led to better conditions for migrant workers.

Women, too, fought against inequalities in the years following the war. In the 1950s and 1960s many women in the work force received lower pay than men in the same job. Groups such as the National Organization of Women helped to change these inequalities. In 1964 the Civil Rights Act forbade discrimination on the basis of gender and race. In 1972 the Equal Employment Opportunity Act required employers to give equal pay to men and women for equal work. Their struggles are not over yet, but black Americans, Hispanic Americans, and women have made great strides on the road to equality.

In 1965 hundreds of demonstrators marched from Selma to Montgomery, Alabama, to draw attention to the plight of southern blacks who had been denied the right to vote.

The readings in this unit focus on the call for equality voiced by Americans long denied equal rights and opportunities.

■ In an interview United Farm Workers leader **Cesar Chavez** describes the creation of the union flag.
■ In a stirring public speech civil rights leader **Dr. Martin Luther King, Jr.**, voices his dream of an America that is truly free.
■ Attorney and Congresswoman **Geraldine Ferraro** speaks of the need for women leaders.

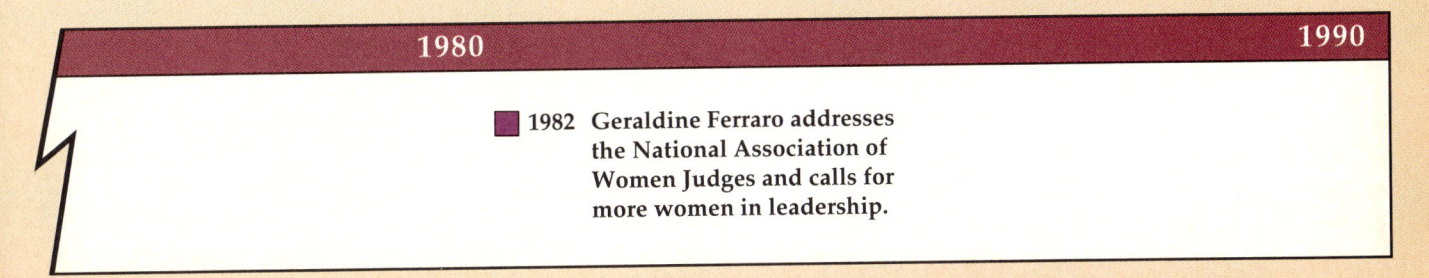

1980 — 1990

■ 1982 Geraldine Ferraro addresses the National Association of Women Judges and calls for more women in leadership.

The Black Eagle Is Born

" We needed an emblem...."
Cesar Chavez

Cesar Chavez's parents lost their farm when he was 10 years old. His family members took jobs as migrant workers.

Following the harvest is a way of life for America's migrant farm workers. Low wages, harsh working conditions, and little education mean chances for a better life are often out of reach for the workers and their families. In 1962 Cesar Chavez began to organize the grape pickers in California into a union. In this reading Chavez describes the creation of a flag for the union, which was first called the National Farm Workers Association.

Richard: brother of Cesar Chavez

Fresno: city in central California

Manuel: brother of Cesar Chavez

We needed an emblem for the Union, a flag that people could see. Many ideas were suggested, but we wanted something that the people could make themselves, and something that had some impact. We didn't want a tractor or a crossed shovel and hoe or a guy with a hoe or pruning shears. I liked the Mexican eagle with a snake in its mouth, but it was too hard to draw.

It was **Richard** who suggested drawing an eagle with square lines, an eagle anyone could make, with five steps in the wings. I chose the colors, red with a black eagle on a white circle.

Red and black flags are used for strikes in Mexico. They mean a union....

We wanted to have the flag ready for our first convention coming up in **Fresno**, so **Manuel** volunteered to make the first one. He's not an artist, but it looked like an eagle, except that the neck looked like a snake. We still kid him about that one....

1962			
1962 Cesar Chavez begins to organize migrant farm workers and other farm laborers in California.	**1965** Farm workers strike against grape growers and call for a national boycott of grapes.		**1970** The grape boycott ends when growers negotiate with workers' union. Lettuce boycott begins.

Our first convention was held on September 30, 1962, in an abandoned theater in Fresno. . . .

There was a big screen in the theater, and our huge flag covered most of it. The flag itself was covered with paper. I wanted Manuel to pull the cord, so I could see the reaction of the people as it was unveiled.

When the eagle appeared, everyone gasped. You could hear it. A few were so shocked we lost them. They thought we were **Communists**. Some commented that the eagle should be gold and the background light blue. Others complained it looked like the **Nazi banner**. I said, "It's what you want to see in it. To me it looks like a strong, beautiful sign of hope."

Manuel was more eloquent. He explained that the black eagle signified the dark situation in which the worker finds himself, the white circle signified hope and aspirations, and the red background indicated the toil and sacrifice that the Association and its members would have to contribute in order to gain justice for the farm workers.

And then he said, "When that . . . eagle flies, the problems of the farm workers will be solved!"

Communists: people supporting a system of government in which the state owns everything

Nazi banner: flag of the nationalist German workers' party that brought Hitler to power

Cesar Chavez remains active in the fight for social justice. He took part in the March for Peace, Jobs and Justice in California in 1988.

La Causa is the name given to the movement to organize migrant farm workers. These efforts were carried beyond California to farm workers in other states. Chavez organized more than 10,000 farm workers in the United States. Today Cesar Chavez continues the struggle to organize workers to stand up for their rights. He fights to win decent wages, job security, and better living and working conditions for the men, women, and children who follow the harvests.

Reprinted from *Cesar Chavez, Autobiography of La Causa*, pp. 173–75, by Jacques E. Levy, by permission of W. W. Norton & Company, Inc. Copyright © 1975 by Jacques E. Levy.

1973 The union name changes to United Farm Workers of America. The grape boycott is renewed.

1978 Boycotts of lettuce and grapes end.

I Have a Dream

" When we let freedom ring, . . . all of God's children . . . will be able to join hands and sing. . . ."
Martin Luther King, Jr.

Martin Luther King, Jr., received the Nobel Peace Prize in 1964 for his dedication to nonviolence in the civil rights movement.

In the 1950s and 1960s many Americans joined a civil rights movement to work for equal rights for black Americans. Martin Luther King, Jr., became the leader of a group that called for peaceful but direct protest against racial **discrimination**. On a hot August day in 1963, he addressed more than 200,000 men, women, and children who had gathered at the Lincoln Memorial in Washington, D.C.

discrimination: the act of showing prejudice by treating in a less favorable way

score: group of twenty

momentous decree: important order

manacles: handcuffs

languished: suffering

appalling: terrible

promissory note: written agreement

fall heir: inherit

Five **score** years ago, a great American, in whose symbolic shadow we stand, signed the Emancipation Proclamation. This **momentous decree** came as a great beacon light of hope to millions of Negro slaves who had been seared in the flames of withering injustice. It came as a joyous daybreak to end the long night of captivity.

But one hundred years later, we must face the tragic fact that the Negro is still not free. One hundred years later, the life of the Negro is still sadly crippled by the **manacles** of segregation and the chains of discrimination. One hundred years later, the Negro lives on a lonely island of poverty in the midst of a vast ocean of material prosperity. One hundred years later, the Negro is still **languished** in the corners of American society and finds himself an exile in his own land. So we have come here today to dramatize an **appalling** condition.

In a sense we have come to our nation's Capitol to cash a check. When the architects of our republic wrote the magnificent words of the Constitution and the Declaration of Independence, they were signing a **promissory note** to which every American was to **fall heir**. This note

1955

1955 Martin Luther King, Jr., leads the Montgomery, Alabama, bus boycott.

1960 Sit-ins are used by black Americans in the South to protest segregated lunch counters.

was a promise that all men would be guaranteed the **unalienable** rights of life, liberty, and the pursuit of happiness.

It is obvious today that America has **defaulted** on this promissory note insofar as her citizens of color are concerned. Instead of honoring this sacred obligation, America has given the Negro people a bad check; a check which has come back marked "insufficient funds." But we refuse to believe that the bank of justice is bankrupt. We refuse to believe that there are insufficient funds in the great vaults of opportunity of this nation. So we have come to cash this check—a check that will give us upon demand the riches of freedom and the security of justice. We have also come to this **hallowed** spot to remind America of the fierce urgency of *now*. This is no time to engage in the luxury of cooling off or to take the tranquilizing drug of **gradualism**. *Now* is the time to make real the promises of Democracy. *Now* is the time to rise from the dark and **desolate** valley of segregation to the sunlit path of racial justice. *Now* is the time to open the doors of opportunity to all of God's children. *Now* is the time to lift our nation from the quicksands of racial injustice to the solid rock of brotherhood.

It would be fatal for the nation to overlook the urgency of the moment and to underestimate the determination of the Negro. This sweltering summer of the Negro's **legitimate** discontent will not pass until there is an invigorating autumn of freedom and equality. 1963 is not an end, but a beginning. Those who hope that the Negro needed to blow off steam and will now be content will have a

unalienable: cannot be taken away

defaulted: failed to pay

hallowed: honored

gradualism: method of reaching a goal step by step

desolate: miserable

legitimate: lawful; reasonable

In 1963 King organized a peaceful demonstration in Birmingham, Alabama, to protest the city's racial discrimination. The demonstrators were met by police with dogs and fire hoses.

| 1963 Over 200,000 people rally in Washington, D.C., to protest racial discrimination. | 1964 Civil Rights Act passes. King receives the Nobel Peace Prize. | 1968 Martin Luther King, Jr., is assassinated. |

113

Until the government passed laws forbidding it, many states had separate public facilities for blacks and whites. This included drinking fountains, restrooms, and even telephone booths.

rude awakening if the Nation returns to business as usual. There will be neither rest nor tranquility in America until the Negro is granted his citizenship rights. The whirlwinds of revolt will continue to shake the foundations of our Nation until the bright day of justice **emerges**.

But there is something that I must say to my people who stand on the warm **threshold** which leads into the palace of justice. In the process of gaining our rightful place we must not be guilty of wrongful deeds. Let us not seek to satisfy our thirst for freedom by drinking from the cup of bitterness and hatred.

We must forever conduct our struggle on the high plane of dignity and discipline. We must not allow our creative protest to **degenerate** into physical violence. Again and again we must rise to the majestic heights of meeting physical force with soul force. The marvelous new **militancy** which has engulfed the Negro community must not lead us to a distrust of all white people, for many of our white brothers, as evidenced by their presence here today, have come to realize that their destiny is tied up with our destiny and their freedom is **inextricably** bound to our freedom. We cannot walk alone.

And as we walk, we must make the pledge that we shall march ahead. We cannot turn back. There are those who are asking the **devotees** of civil rights, "when will you be satisfied?" We can never be satisfied as long as the Negro is the victim of the unspeakable horrors of police brutality. We can never be satisfied as long as our bodies, heavy with the fatigue of travel, cannot gain lodging in the motels of the highways and the hotels of the cities. We cannot be satisfied as long as the Negro's basic mobility is from a smaller **ghetto** to a larger one. We can never be satisfied as long as a Negro in Mississippi cannot vote and a Negro in New York believes he has nothing for which to vote. No, no we are not satisfied, and we will not be satisfied until justice rolls down like waters and **righteousness** like a mighty stream.

emerges: becomes visible

threshold: doorway

degenerate: sink into a lower or worse condition

militancy: aggressive behavior or spirit

inextricably: cannot be untangled

devotees: people strongly committed to something

ghetto: slum

righteousness: goodness

I am not **unmindful** that some of you have come here out of great trials and **tribulations**. Some of you have come fresh from narrow jail cells. Some of you have come from areas where your **quest** for freedom left you battered by the storms of persecution and staggered by the winds of police brutality. You have been the veterans of creative suffering. Continue to work with the faith that unearned suffering is **redemptive**.

Go back to Mississippi, go back to Alabama, go back to South Carolina, go back to Georgia, go back to Louisiana, go back to the slums and ghettos of our northern cities, knowing that somehow this situation can and will be changed. Let us not **wallow** in the valley of despair.

I say to you today, my friends, that in spite of the difficulties and **frustrations** of the moment I still have a dream. It is a dream deeply rooted in the American dream. . . .

I have a dream that one day on the red hills of Georgia the sons of former slaves and the sons of former slaveowners will be able to sit down together at the table of brotherhood.

I have a dream that one day even the state of Mississippi, a desert state sweltering with the heat of injustice and **oppression**, will be transformed into an oasis of freedom and justice.

I have a dream that my four little children will one day live in a nation where they will not be judged by the color of their skin but by the content of their character.

I have a dream today.

I have a dream that one day the state of Alabama, whose governor's lips are presently dripping

unmindful: unaware

tribulations: troubles

quest: search

redemptive: worthwhile over time

wallow: remain helpless

frustrations: feelings of insecurity and dissatisfaction

oppression: harsh rule

Peaceful civil rights demonstrators were confronted by armed National Guard troops and tanks when they marched through Memphis in 1968.

Jubilant bus riders point to a sign soon to be removed. In 1956 the U.S. Supreme Court banned segregation on all public transportation.

interposition: action by which a state tries to interfere with federal law

nullification: action by which a state tries to prevent the enforcement of a federal law

exalted: raised high

hew: cut; chop

discords: disagreements

prodigious: very great; marvelous

curvaceous: having curves

with the words of **interposition** and **nullification**, will be transformed into a situation where little black boys and black girls will be able to join hands with little white boys and white girls and walk together as sisters and brothers.

I have a dream today.

I have a dream that one day every valley shall be **exalted**, every hill and mountain shall be made low, the rough places will be made plains, and the crooked places will be made straight, and the glory of the Lord shall be revealed. . . .

This is our hope. This is the faith with which I return to the South. With this faith we will be able to **hew** out of the mountain of despair a stone of hope. With this faith we will be able to transform the jangling **discords** of our nation into a beautiful symphony of brotherhood. With this faith we will be able to work together, to pray together, to struggle together, to go to jail together, to stand up for freedom together, knowing that we will be free one day.

This will be the day when all of God's children will be able to sing with new meaning "My country 'tis of thee, sweet land of liberty, of thee I sing. Land where my fathers died, land of the pilgrim's pride, from every mountainside, let freedom ring."

And if America is to be a great nation this must become true. So let freedom ring from the **prodigious** hilltops of New Hampshire. Let freedom ring from the mighty mountains of New York. Let freedom ring from the heightening Alleghenies of Pennsylvania!

Let freedom ring from the snowcapped Rockies of Colorado!

Let freedom ring from the **curvaceous** peaks of California!

But not only that; let freedom ring from Stone Mountain of Georgia!

Let freedom ring from Lookout Mountain of Tennessee!

Let freedom ring from every hill and mole hill of Mississippi. From every mountainside, let freedom ring.

When we let freedom ring, when we let it ring from every village and every **hamlet**, from every state and every city, we will be able to speed up that day when all of God's children, black men and white men, Jews and **Gentiles**, Protestants and Catholics, will be able to join hands and sing in the words of the old Negro spiritual, "Free at last! free at last! thank God almighty, we are free at last!"

hamlet: very small village

Gentiles: non-Jews

In 1963 King and other civil rights leaders organized the Freedom March in Washington, D.C. More than 200,000 people marched to show their support for equal rights.

Martin Luther King, Jr., did not live to see his dream fulfilled. He was shot and killed on April 4, 1968, while in Memphis, Tennessee. People everywhere mourned his death. Today, black Americans have come closer to the dream but are still working to achieve equality. A national holiday, the third Monday of January, was established in 1983 to honor the memory of Martin Luther King, Jr.

From *The Civil Rights Reader*, ed. Leon Friedman (New York: Walker and Co., 1967), pp. 110–13. "I Have a Dream," copyright © 1963 by Martin Luther King, Jr. Reprinted by permission of Joan Daves.

Women in Leadership

" . . . women in leadership positions make a real difference in the way our society works."

          Geraldine A. Ferraro

Geraldine Ferraro made history in 1984 as the first female vice-presidential candidate for a major American political party.

discrimination: showing prejudice by treating in a less favorable way

district attorney: government lawyer who works in a particular part of a city

Queens: a section of New York City

motion: request for a ruling from a court or a judge

ghetto: slum

Fordham: university in New York City

prestigious: successful; famous

culminated: ended

Yet another group—the largest in America—joined the battle against **discrimination**. American women added their voices to the call for equality. Their words were echoed by leaders such as New York Congresswoman Geraldine Ferraro. She stated that American society would be better if women were allowed to have a fair share of leadership roles. She tells why in a speech to the National Association of Women Judges in 1982.

When I was an assistant **district attorney** in **Queens** it used to make me terribly nervous to get up and argue a **motion** in front of one judge. So you can imagine how I feel standing up here in front of hundreds of judges.

Of course, I am not here today to argue. But I am here to plead a case. My case is that women in leadership positions make a real difference in the way our society works. And I believe that women like us must continue to make that difference.

All of our futures, and our daughters' futures, are at stake.

I am talking about the future of every woman, from the migrant farm worker or **ghetto** mother to United States Supreme Court Justice Sandra Day O'Connor, a founder of this organization and your honoree earlier today.

I speak to you as a Member of Congress who has not forgotten that she is a lawyer who never forgets she is a woman. How could I?

I was one of just two women in my law class at **Fordham** in the late 50s. In 1960, five job interviews at one of our **prestigious** New York law firms **culminated** with a "you're

1972			
1972 Congress passes the Equal Rights Amendment.	1974 Janet Gray Hayes of San José, California, is elected the first woman mayor of a major city.	1981 Sandra Day O'Connor becomes the first woman justice of the United States Supreme Court.

terrific, but we're not hiring any women this year." As a **bureau chief** in the **DA's** office many years later, I learned that I was being paid less than men with similar responsibilities. When I asked why, I was told "you don't really need the money, Gerry, you've got a husband."

Getting to Congress wasn't easy either. The biggest problem in running as a woman, if by some quirk you get the **organization endorsement**, is raising money. I remember going from bank to bank in 1978 for a campaign loan and being told that my husband had to **cosign**. Forget that I was a lawyer with a good deal of trial experience. Just remember that even if I wanted my husband to sign, I couldn't because I would be in violation of the **FEC** laws. . . .

As recently as two weeks ago, Capitol Hill police stopped me at four different locations, the last when I entered the House for a roll call vote, and demanded identification. Four years I've been walking in and out of those **hallowed** halls. Clearly, they found it more difficult to recognize me—one of just 20 women in the House—than any of the 415 men.

Yes, the **"old boy network"** is alive and well and living in our courthouses and our legislatures and our boardrooms. As women, we still have to be better than men at most of the things we do, we have to work harder, and we have to prove our worth over and over and over again. . . .

Look at the facts. More women than men are poor and it is harder for them to escape poverty. Indeed, more and more women are struggling to support children alone, earning 59 cents for each dollar a man earns. . . . Cuts in **domestic programs**, seemingly **gender-neutral**, actually hit women and children twice as hard as they do men because women are the greatest number of **recipients**. Ninety-two percent of the participants in Aid for Dependent Children are women and children. Sixty-six percent of the recipients of **subsidized** housing are women. Sixty-nine percent of food stamp recipients are women. Sixty-one percent of **Medicaid** recipients are women.

The women's movement gained strength during the 1960s and 1970s. Followers worked for equal rights and opportunities.

bureau chief: head of a department

DA's: district attorney's

organization endorsement: political party approval

cosign: accept legal responsibility for another's debt

FEC: Federal Election Commission

hallowed: honored

"old boy network": group of men who help one another and exclude others

domestic programs: government's plans to help its own people

gender-neutral: having the same effect on women as on men

recipients: people who receive

subsidized: supported with government money

Medicaid: public health plan that pays some of the medical expenses for people with little or no income

---

1984

1982 Congresswoman Geraldine Ferraro addresses the National Association of Women Judges.

1983 Sally Ride becomes the first American woman in space.

1984 Geraldine Ferraro becomes the first female vice-presidential candidate of a major party.

119

In 1981 Sandra Day O'Connor was chosen as the first woman to serve as a U.S. Supreme Court justice.

And why are women dependent on federal help? It is not because they are lazier than men or less moral than men. Or less intelligent.

Women are in greater need because they often have less education. They are the ones who must care for the children. They must work part-time or in **menial** jobs and they get paid less for the work that they do. . . .

I did a little research the other day. I wanted to find out how many women in America earn more than $60,000 a year. I picked that number, frankly, because that is what I, as a member of Congress, earn. I learned that there are only 18,000 women in the entire United States, working full-time who earn more than $60,000. We represent just one-tenth of one percent of all the women who work full-time in America. By contrast, 885,000 men, 2.1 percent of full-time male workers, are in the $60,000-plus bracket. . . .

I said earlier that I believe women in leadership make a real difference in our society. Now, there are really two reasons why there needs to be more women in leadership. . . .

The first reason could be called the "Me-First" reason. We are smart, we worked hard, we deserve this job, we are entitled to it and we will do anything necessary to get and keep it. Women of merit do indeed deserve their fair share of society's rewards, a share previously denied to us only because we were women.

The second reason, though, is more important. Women leaders are different. Despite our frequent political and **philosophical** differences, there are certain generalizations that can be made about women judges and women legislators. We care more about other women. We show more concern for children. We try to resolve controversies by cooperation, rather than conflict. . . . In short, men often worry more about rules and processes. Women often worry more about outcomes.

We have an obligation to use our unique **perspective** when we make the laws, as I do, and interpret the laws, as you do.

Your distinguished honoree, Justice O'Connor, has made this kind of difference on the Supreme Court. . . .

When women are named to federal courts, there is pressure to name them to state and municipal benches as well. . . . When women become judges, when more and more women graduate from law school, not only government, but private enterprise, has to realize that women are a force to be dealt with and treated with respect. . . .

I didn't go to Washington to represent the women of this nation. But if I don't, who will? I ran, and

menial: low value

philosophical: general beliefs and attitudes

perspective: point of view

was elected, not as a **feminist**, but as a lawyer. And as a lawyer I can argue more effectively for **equity** and fairness for all Americans. . . .

As women we are a majority, but as judges and legislators we are still an all-too-small minority in America. As a minority, our responsibilities—to our sex, our professions, and our nation—are heavy ones. A majority may have the luxury of being a "**silent majority**." A minority in defense of its rights must speak up.

As members of a minority we have a responsibility to be role-models for all women. As a minority, we bear the burden of expressing the minority viewpoint and keeping it ever before the American public. Our responsibilities are heavy but they are not **oppressive**. We have an opportunity as well as an obligation —an opportunity to help create a better society for all Americans, men and women.

Madam Justices, I rest my case. The verdict is yours.

feminist: one who promotes women's rights

equity: justice

"silent majority": a great number of people who do not publicly express their views

oppressive: overwhelming

In 1977 thousands of women marched in Washington, D.C., to mark the fifty-seventh anniversary of the Nineteenth Amendment.

Geraldine Ferraro gave her speech at a dinner honoring Sandra Day O'Connor, the first woman to be named a Supreme Court justice. Just two years later Ferraro made history when she was nominated to be the Democratic party's vice-presidential candidate in 1984. Her role as a candidate has been a model for women in politics.

From *Representative American Speeches, 1982–1983*, ed. Owen Peterson (New York: H. W. Wilson Co., 1983), pp. 199–207. Reprinted by permission of Geraldine Ferraro.

INDEX

African Americans. *See* Black Americans.
Aid for Dependent Children, 119
Alabama, 79, 115
Albany, New York, 48–49
Aldrich, Mrs. Alfred Proctor, 54–57
Allies, 86–87, 100–107
American Expeditionary Forces, 86
American Revolution, 31–35
Ames, Iowa, 79
Anthony, Susan B., 72–75
Appomattox, 58–61
Arkansas, 77
Atlantic Ocean, 16
Azores, 7

belief systems, 18–21, 28–31, 34–35, 46–49, 52–61, 66–67, 72–83, 88–89, 96–99, 106–107, 110–121
Bennett, Joseph, 20–21
Berlin, Germany, 87
Black Americans, 28, 34–35, 46–49, 76–79, 98–99, 112–117
botany, 79
Bullitt, William C., 89

Cadiz, 9, 11
California, 38–41, 64, 65, 96–98, 110–111, 116
Canada, 48–49, 74
Canary Islands, 4, 9
Carver, George Washington, 76–79
Carver, James, 76–78
Carver, Moses, 76
Cascade Mountains, 41
Castañeda, Pedro de, 12–13
Castile, 7, 9
Cathay, 5
cattle, 42–45, 68–69
Central America, 12
Central Pacific Railroad, 64–65
characteristics of place, 4–13, 16–17, 38–45, 80–83, 88–93, 106–107, 110–111
Chateau Thierry, 86
Chavez, Cesar, 110–111
Chicago, Illinois, 80–83
China, 4
Cicuye, 12–13
citizens, role of. *See* leadership.
citizenship, 72–75, 118–121
civil rights, 46–49, 66–67, 72–83, 106–107, 110–121. *See also* social conflict.
Civil War, 52–61, 76
clothing, 68–69
coal-miners, 88–89
colonial army, 32–35
colonialism, 4–13, 16–25, 28–35
colonies, 16–25, 28–31

Colorado, 116
Columbia River, 45
Columbus, Christopher, 4–8
concentration camp, 106–107
Confederate States of America, 52–61
Congress, U.S., 33, 83, 118–120
Continental Army, 32–35
Coronado, Francisco de, 12–13
correspondents, war, 100
cowboys, 68–69
customs and traditions, 18–21

Dachau, 106–107
D-day, 100–105
defense work, 96–99
Diamond Grove, Missouri, 76
Dillon, Sidney, 64–65
discrimination. *See* civil rights.

economic system, 22–25, 80–83, 88–93, 96–99, 110–111, 119–120
education, 18, 76–79, 110
election, 72–75
Elkhorn River, 43
England, 28–31, 86, 102
Europe, 4, 86–87, 100–107
expansion, 38–45, 64–69
exploration, 4–13, 42–45

factory, aircraft, 96–99
Fayetteville, Arkansas, 77
FEC (Federal Election Commission) laws, 119
Fellenz, Colonel Walter J., 106–107
Ferdinand, king of Spain, 4, 7, 9
Ferrando, Don. *See* Ferdinand.
Ferraro, Geraldine, 118–121
Fordham University, 118
Fort Laramie, Wyoming, 45
Fort Scott, Kansas, 77
Fortunate Islands, 9
France, 86–87, 100–105
Franklin, Benjamin, 28–31
Frémont, John, 38
frontier, 38–45, 64–69

Gannett, Deborah Sampson, 32–33
Georgia, 54, 115–116
Germany, 86–87, 102, 106–107
Gettysburg, Battle of, 52–53
gold, 12–13, 38–41
golden spike, 64–65
government, 72–75, 80–83, 90–93
  principles, 28–31, 110–121
  structure, 72–75, 112–121
Grant, Jehu, 34–35
Grant, Ulysses S., 57–61, 64
Grapes of Wrath, The, 93
Great Britain, 28–31, 86, 102
Great Depression, 88–93

Great Plains, 90
Guanahani. *See* San Salvador.

Haley, John, 52–53
Harding, Lieutenant Phelps, 86–87
heritage, 12–13, 18–21, 34–35, 66–67, 76–79, 96–99, 110–121
H-hour, 103
Hispaniola, 5–7
Holocaust, 106–107
homestead community, 88–89
Honduras, 7
Hoovervilles, 91
House of Commons, 30
House of Lords, 30
Hunt, Judge Ward, 72–75
Hunter, General, 56–57

indentured servants, 22–25
Indianola, Iowa, 78
Indians. *See* Native Americans.
Indies, 4–7
innovation and technology, 8–11, 38–41, 52–53, 64–65, 80–83, 96–99
invasion, 100–105
Iowa, 78–79
Iowa State College, 79
Isabella, queen of Spain, 4, 7

James, W. S., 68–69
Jews, 106–107, 117
Jones, William, 46–49
Jungle, The, 80–83

Kansas, 13, 77
King, Martin Luther, Jr., 112–117
Knight, Amelia Stewart, 42–45
Ku Klux Klan, 76

La Causa, 111
labor, 22–25, 38–41, 64–65, 80–83, 88–93, 96–99, 110–111
labor unions, 110–111
laws, need for, 72–75, 80–83, 110–121
leadership, 58–61, 66–67, 72–79, 88–89, 96–99, 110–121
Lee, Robert E., 52, 58–61
lifestyles, 16–25, 38–49, 54–57, 66–69, 76–83, 88–93, 96–99, 110–121
Lincoln Memorial, 112
Lisbon, Portugal, 8
location, 4–13, 38–45, 64–65, 100–105
Louisiana, 115

Mann, Herman, 32–33
maps
  colonies
    American Colonies, 1776, 26
    Northern Colonies, 1750, 14

maps (continued)
  exploration routes
    Three New World Explorers, 1492–1541, 2
  military
    The Civil War, 1861–1865, 50
    Europe in World War II, 94
    The Normandy Invasion, 101
    Sherman's March Through the South, 55
  miscellaneous
    The American West, 1870, 62
    Main Routes of the Underground Railroad, 36
    The United States, 1900, 70
    The United States During the 1930s, 84
    United States Population, 1989, 108
march to the sea, 54–57
Massachusetts Bay Colony, 17–19
Massasoit, 17
Meat Inspection Act, 83
meat-packing industry, 80–83
Medicaid, 119
Memphis, Tennessee, 117
Mexican War, 58
Mexico, 12–13, 110
migrant workers, 90–93, 110–111. See also labor.
mining, 38–41, 88–89
Minneapolis, Kansas, 77
Mississippi, 114, 115, 117
Missouri, 42, 76–77
Mittelberger, Gottlieb, 22–25
movement of people, 16–25, 38–49, 64–65, 90–93, 106–107
Munich, Germany, 106

National Association of Women Judges, 118
National Farm Workers Association, 110–111
Native Americans, 4–13, 16–17, 40, 42, 66–67
Nazi Party, 106–107, 111
Nebraska, 43, 64
Negroes. See Black Americans.
Neosho, Missouri, 77
Neuman, Charlcia, 96–99
New England, 16–21
New Hampshire, 116
New Mexico, 13
New York, 49, 64–66, 72, 114, 118
Nineteenth Amendment, 75
Normandy, 100–105

O'Connor, Sandra Day, 118, 120, 121
Okinawa, 105
Oklahoma, 13, 91

Omaha, Nebraska, 64
Oregon, 42–45
Oregon Territory, 42–45
Oregon Trail, 42–45

Parliament, British, 28–31
Pearl Harbor, 96
Pecos, New Mexico (Cicuye), 12–13
Peel, William, 46–49
Pennsylvania, 22–25, 28–29, 52–53, 116
pension, 33–35
Perkins, Elisha Douglass, 38–41
Philadelphia, 22, 28, 47
Pickett, General George, 53
"Pickett's Charge", 53
Pilgrims, 16–17
plantation, 16
Plymouth Colony, 16–17
polio, 88
production. See labor.
Promontory Point, Utah, 64
pueblo, 12–13
Pulitzer Prize, 100
Pure Food and Drug Act, 83
Puritans, 18–21
Pyle, Ernie, 100–105

Quakers, 88–89
Queens, New York, 118

railroad, 64–65
rebellion. See war.
Red Cloud, Chief, 66–67
relationships—people and place, 34–35, 46–49, 88–89, 90–93
"relief", 88–89
revolution. See war.
Revolution, The, 75
Revolutionary War, 31–35
Rhode Island, 34
Rio Grande Valley, 90
Rochester, New York, 72
Roosevelt, Eleanor, 88–89
Roosevelt, Franklin D., 88
Roosevelt, Theodore, 83
Round Top (Gettysburg), 52
rules. See laws.

Sabbath, 18, 20–21
Sacramento, California, 38
Sacramento River, 41
St. Mihiel, 86–87
Salkehatchie River, 54
Sampson, Deborah, 32–33
San Francisco, California, 41, 64–65
San Salvador, 4
Savannah, Georgia, 54
scarcity, 54–57, 88–93, 96–99. See also supply and demand.
Seminary Ridge (Gettysburg), 52

serf, 24
settlement, 16–25, 38–49, 64–67
seven cities of gold, 12–13
Sherman, General William T., 54–57
Sierra Nevada, 40, 41
Simpson College, 78
Sinclair, Upton, 80–83
Sioux. See Native Americans.
slaves and slavery, 34–35, 46–49. See also Black Americans.
social class and systems, 18–25, 32–35, 46–49, 72–79, 90–93, 106–107, 110–121
social conflict, 8–13, 46–49, 66–67, 72–83, 106–107, 110–121
South America, 11
South Carolina, 54–57, 115
Southwest (American), 13
Spain, 4, 6–13
SS (Schutzstaffel), 106–107
Stamp Act, 28–31
Still, William, 46–49
stockyards, 80–83
Sumner, Mary Osgood, 18–19, 21
supply and demand, 22–25, 28–31, 38–41, 80–83, 86–93, 96–99, 110–117. See also scarcity.
Supreme Court, 118, 120, 121
Sutter's Mill, 40

taxation, 28–31
technology, 52–53, 64–65, 96–99
Tennessee, 117
Terry, Peggy, 90–93
Texas, 13, 90
Teyas, 13
torrid zone, 10
Townshend Acts, 31
transcontinental railroad, 64–65
Tropic of Cancer, 10
Tuskegee Institute, 79

Underground Railroad, 46–49
Union forces, 52–61
Union Pacific Railroad, 64–65
Utah, 64

values. See belief systems.
Vespucci, Amerigo, 8–11
Vigilance Committee, 48
Virginia, 52
voting, 72–75

WACS (Women's Army Corps), 98
war, 12–13, 32–35, 52–61, 86–87, 96–107
wars, American
  Civil War, 52–61, 76
  Mexican War, 58
  Revolutionary War, 32–35

123

wars, American (continued)
    World War I, 86–87
    World War II, 96–107
Washington, D.C., 112
Webster's Elementary Spelling Book, 77
West Virginia, 88–89
westward movement, 38–45, 64–67

Winslow, Edward, 16–17
women in history
    Aldrich, Mrs. Alfred Proctor, 54–57
    Anthony, Susan B., 72–75
    Ferraro, Geraldine, 118–121
    Knight, Amelia Stewart, 42–45
    Neuman, Charlcia, 96–99
    Roosevelt, Eleanor, 88–89

women in history (continued)
    Sampson, Deborah, 32–33
    Sumner, Mary Osgood, 18–19, 21
    Terry, Peggy, 90–93
women's rights. *See* civil rights.
World War I, 86–87
World War II, 96–107

Zuñi, 13

PHOTO CREDITS

Table of Contents: iii (top to bottom) Unit 1: North Wind Picture Archives. Unit 2: The Bettmann Archive. Unit 3: The Granger Collection, New York. Unit 4: Historical Pictures Service, Chicago. Unit 5: Art Resource. **iv** (top to bottom) Unit 6: The Bettmann Archive. Unit 7: The Bettmann Archive. Unit 8: Culver Pictures, Inc. Unit 9: Culver Pictures, Inc. Unit 10: Victor Aleman/Black Star.

Introduction: 1: The Bettmann Archive.

Unit One: 3: Historical Pictures Service, Chicago. 4: North Wind Picture Archives. 5: Art Resource. 6: North Wind Picture Archives. 8: Art Resource. 9, 10: North Wind Picture Archives. 12: The Granger Collection, New York. 13: North Wind Picture Archives.

Unit Two: 15: Historical Pictures Service, Chicago. 16: North Wind Picture Archives. 18, 19: The Bettmann Archive. 20, 21: North Wind Picture Archives. 22: The Granger Collection, New York. 23: The Bettmann Archive. 24: The Historical Society of Pennsylvania.

Unit Three: 27: North Wind Picture Archives. 28: The Bettmann Archive. 29, 30, 31: North Wind Picture Archives. 32: Sophia Smith Collection, Smith College. 33: The Bettmann Archive. 34: The Granger Collection, New York.

Unit Four: 37: Scala/Art Resource. 38: Historical Pictures Service, Chicago. 39: Culver Pictures, Inc. 40: The Bettmann Archive. 41: The Granger Collection, New York. 42: North Wind Picture Archives. 43: The Bettmann Archive. 44: National Archives. 45: Culver Pictures, Inc. 46: The Granger Collection, New York. 47: Art Resource. 48 (both): Culver Pictures, Inc. 49: Historical Pictures Service, Chicago.

Unit Five: 51: Scala/Art Resource. 52: North Wind Picture Archives. 53, 54: The Bettmann Archive. 56: North Wind Picture Archives. 57, 58: The Bettmann Archive. 60: North Wind Picture Archives.

Unit Six: 63: North Wind Picture Archives. 64: Culver Pictures, Inc. 65: Scala/Art Resource. 66: The Bettmann Archive. 67: North Wind Picture Archives. 68: Culver Pictures, Inc. 69: (top right) Culver Pictures, Inc.; (bottom and top left) The Bettmann Archive.

Unit Seven: 71: The Granger Collection, New York. 72: Sophia Smith Collection, Smith College. 73: The Bettmann Archive. 74: Sophia Smith Collection, Smith College. 75: The Bettmann Archive. 76: UPI/Bettmann. 77, 78: The Granger Collection, New York. 79: UPI/Bettmann. 80, 81, 82, 83: The Bettmann Archive.

Unit Eight: 85: Culver Pictures, Inc. 86: The Granger Collection, New York. 88, 89: UPI/Bettmann Newsphotos. 90: Culver Pictures, Inc. 91: (top) UPI/Bettmann Newsphotos; (bottom) The Bettmann Archive. 92: (all) The Bettmann Archive. 93: UPI/Bettmann Newsphotos.

Unit Nine: 95: Culver Pictures, Inc. 96, 97, 98: UPI/Bettmann Newsphotos. 99: The Granger Collection, New York. 100: UPI/Bettmann Newsphotos. 102, 103: Culver Pictures, Inc. 104, 105: Robert Capa/Magnum. 106: David Seymour/Magnum. 107: D.B. Owen/Black Star.

Unit Ten: 109: Bob Adelman/Magnum. 110: Bob Fitch/Black Star. 111: Victor Aleman/Black Star. 112: UPI/Bettmann Newsphotos. 113: Charles Moore/Black Star. 114: The Bettmann Archive. 115, 116, 117, 118: UPI/Bettmann Newsphotos. 119: Arthur Tress/Magnum. 121: UPI/Bettmann Newsphotos.